THE ULTIMATE WORLD

BY
CARMEN
TRIPODI

ISBN 978-1-7326977-1-3

Published By:

UltimatePerson.com LLC
P.O. Box 11973
Zephyr Cove, NV 89448

CONTENTS

INTRODUCTION

This book defines a whole new world. It is a world where all people work together as a problem solving team to solve all the world's problems, and to have fun doing it. It is the world of the future.

Imagine . . . No more wars. No more violence. No more poverty. No more racism. No more sexism. No more hate.

At first thought, this all sounds like some sort of dream that can't happen in the real world. Well think again, using the ideas expressed in this book, the world can solve all of its problems, and have fun too. This is because the ideas expressed here are based on science. The scientific method is carefully followed, and the entire book is centered around a new scientific theory of this ultimate world.

The title of this new scientific theory is Ultimate World Theory. Ultimate World Theory, or UW Theory for short, is the scientific theory that solves the world's problems and saves the world.

The Ultimate World Problem

The ultimate problem facing humans, now and forever, is the problem of survival. The universe is a very cold, dark and violent place to live, and human survival is by no means guaranteed. It is as if the same universe that created human life doesn't care whether we survive it or not. Fortunately, we were given brains that can figure things out, and we can use these brains to figure out a solution to the human survival problem.

This problem of human survival can be characterized in terms of two types of threats to survival – natural and artificial. Let us start with the natural threats. The most obvious natural threat comes from the sun which is heating up over time and will eventually burn out, making life on earth uninhabitable along the way. We can be reasonably certain about this because the sun is a star similar to numerous other stars in the universe, and behaves similar to these other stars which heat up and burn out over time. By observing other stars at different points in their life cycle, we can predict the life cycle of the sun with a reasonable amount of accuracy.

See the following chart showing the life cycle of the sun, from its formation as a baby star to its death as a white dwarf, approximately 13 billion years later. We can see that, unfortunately, life on earth has a limited time. This chart points out the approximate time for the end of life on earth. The good news is that this endpoint is about 2.5 billion years from now, which gives us plenty of time to figure out a solution.

Another obvious natural threat to human survival is the limited resources available to support human life in space. Due to the limited life cycle of the sun, we can be reasonably certain that we are eventually going to need to colonize space, and finding the resources to support large scale human life in space is another major problem. Food, water, oxygen, shelter, and other survival necessities are not readily available in space.

Life Cycle of the Sun

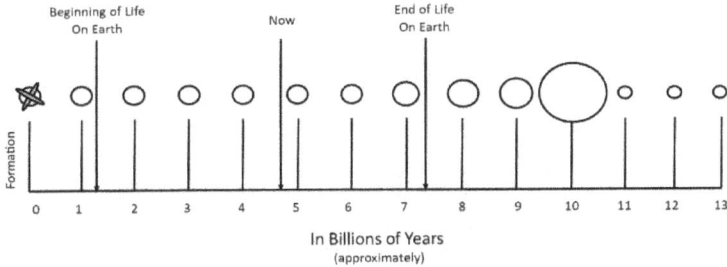

Other less severe natural threats include space objects such as meteors and asteroids, which can harm the earth and its atmosphere upon impact. And there is also the threat of a pandemic of infectious disease, such as the COVID-19 pandemic, that can quickly spread across the world.

Now for the artificial threats (also known as anthropogenic threats). The most obvious artificial threat is the social problem of human conflicts around the world, which manifests itself in terms of war and violence. These conflicts could escalate and lead to self-destruction of the human species.

And there is a long list of other social problems in the world that need to be solved. Some of the major ones are poverty, racism and sexism. Most of these social problems are also conflict related.

A simple way of thinking about the Ultimate World problem is "all the world's problems." This simple problem statement of "all the world's problems" is too vague to be useful, however. A more specific statement of the problem is required to deal with the problem scientifically, which can then lead to a practical solution.

A more specific statement of the Ultimate World problem is "survive the universe using the minimum resources." This more specific statement of the Ultimate World problem is derived directly from the natural threats to survival. *The artificial threats will be dealt with in the process of solving the problems within the natural threats.* This problem solving process is described in detail in Chapter 3 The Practice of The Ultimate World.

When this problem solving process is performed correctly, optimal problem solving performance will be achieved. And since the science of happiness shows us that optimal performance and optimal experience (happiness) are directly linked, maximum world happiness will also be achieved.

So, the Ultimate World problem is hereby defined as "survive the universe using the minimum resources."

The Ultimate World Solution

The Ultimate World problem of "survive the universe using the minimum resources" is an extremely complex problem. It is actually the most complex problem imaginable to humans. This is the bad news.

Now for the good news.

The good news is that there is a solution to the Ultimate World problem. The solution is simple, yet scientific, and is given in the following simple formula:

$$UW = UP_{MAX}$$

where UP stands for Ultimate Person. A basic definition of a UP is a *person who maximizes problem solving skill over time.* The *MAX* subscript stands for the maximum possible number of UPs.

Everything in UW Theory stems from this simple, yet scientific formula. The science underlying this formula is explained in Chapter 2 The Science of The Ultimate World.

A Good Starting Point

The solution to the Ultimate World problem given in this book does not contain all the details. The Ultimate World problem of "survive the universe using minimum resources" is so complex, it is virtually impossible to define all the details all at one time.

The solution given here is just a good starting point for a completely detailed solution to the Ultimate World problem. It is a good starting point because:

> 1) it correctly defines the big issues involved in the Ultimate World solution; and
> 2) it provides a scientific method for defining the remaining details, over time.

A brief statement of the big issues is given below. The method for defining the remaining details is the Ultimate World Scientific Method which is defined in Chapter 2.

The Ultimate World Big Issues

The benefits of knowing big issues are significant. For example: a) by knowing the big issues there is a greater chance of success on the big issues; b) big mistakes (such as the human species going extinct) can be prevented; c) big issues provide guidance to the identification of all the details; and d) big issues are timeless – they do not change much over time and therefore, once they are defined, they can be relied upon for a long period of time, ideally infinity.

There are three big issues involved in solving the Ultimate World problem:

1) the Ultimate World context - the Ultimate World context is a big issue because it serves as a baseline, or reference point, for analysis of all the issues. The Ultimate World context is detailed in Chapter 1.

2) the science of the Ultimate World - the science of the Ultimate World is a big issue because the scientific method is the best method to identify the correct solution to the Ultimate World problem. The science of the Ultimate World is detailed in Chapter 2.

3) the practice of the Ultimate World. The practice of the Ultimate World is a big issue because of the need to produce results by solving actual problems. The practice of the Ultimate World is detailed in Chapter 3.

The remainder of the outline to this book includes: Chapter 4 Summary of The Ultimate World Hypotheses; Chapter 5 Summary of The Ultimate World Predictions; and Chapter 6 Ultimate World Experiments.

Contributions To The World

Ultimate World Theory makes a long list of contributions to the world. Here are the primary ones:

1) *A scientific solution to the human survival problem –* by defining the "do or die" actions for human survival of the universe, it defines how to save the human species from extinction and thereby saves the world.

2) *A scientific solution to all the world's problems–* by defining the solution to all the rest of the world's problems, including the most serious problems that never get solved such as war, violence, and poverty.

3) *How to save the world and have fun doing it* – by defining a new scientific process for maximizing problem solving performance and happiness, for both individuals and groups.

4) *Contributions to science*, including: a new knowledge type; and a new scientific method for identifying the actions necessary for human survival of the universe.

5) *Scientific predictions for the future of the world*, including: the future of individual people; the future of society as a whole; the future of technology; the future economy; and the future of communication.

6) *A whole lot more.*

How To Read This Book

This book is presented in the form of a scientific argument. It is not necessarily a pleasure read. It is structured in terms of the Basic Scientific Method which is the standard for credible science. An overview of The Basic Scientific Method is given in Appendix A1, page 195.

For readers new to science, it is recommended to first read Appendix A1. For scientists, it is also recommended to first read Appendix A1, so that we can all be on the same page. After reading Appendix A1, it is then recommended to proceed to Chapter 1 entitled The Ultimate World Context.

This book serves as the textbook for the online course on Ultimate World Theory available at www.ultimateperson.com. This online course, entitled Ultimate World Course, includes supplemental lessons and quizzes, all of which enhance learning. Completion of this course certifies students as Ultimate Person Experts.

A beginner on-line course is also available at www.ultimateperson.com, entitled Ultimate Person Course. The textbook for this beginner course is a companion book entitled *The Ultimate Person.* It is recommended that all students take this beginner course before taking the advanced course on Ultimate World Theory. This beginner course teaches the essential skill of *maximum problem solving skill over time,* and certifies students as an official Ultimate Person.

1

THE ULTIMATE WORLD CONTEXT

The Ultimate World Context is a big issue because it serves as a reference point or baseline for analysis and evaluation of all the issues. Using different contexts to deal with a problem is like comparing apples and oranges, and makes analysis and evaluation of the issues difficult and confusing.

Around the world, there are a lot of different personalities, and a lot of different perspectives on life. These different perspectives are derived from the different cultural backgrounds. While all this diversity is wonderful, when it comes to problem solving, we all need to be on the same page, and the Ultimate World context puts everyone in the world on the same page. We need unity in addition to diversity when solving problems, especially the problem of human survival.

The Ultimate World Context is based on three main points.

Point #1 The most important issue facing humans is the survival of the species.

Point #2 The best way to address the issue of survival of the species is by means of a problem solving approach.

Point #3 The best way to find the correct solutions to the human survival problems is by means of the scientific method.

Point #1 The most important issue facing humans is survival of the species.

Why is survival of the species the most important issue facing humans all around the world? First of all, it is common sense that human survival is the most important issue. We all want people to live long and prosper, and we all feel bad when people die. It is as if this moral code is built into our genetic code.

But let's take a look at what it will actually mean if the human species goes extinct. Here are the primary implications of human extinction:

1) an inconceivably large number of human lives would be lost by not being born;
2) the significance of the lives of all the people alive today would be lost;
3) the significance of the lives of all the billions of our ancestors would be lost;
4) everything in history associated with being human, including all culture, all art, and all science would be lost.

Overall, human extinction would be the most catastrophic event imaginable to humans. It would mean the complete end of the human species. If one is not convinced of the importance of human survival from a strictly rational point of view, then one should be convinced from a strictly emotional point of view. Everyone should be convinced from both rational and emotional points of view.

Point #2 The best way to address the issue of survival of the species is by means of a problem solving approach

Why is a problem solving approach the best way to address the issue of the survival of the species? The problem solving approach is the best for two main reasons: 1) there are problems (namely, threats to survival); and 2) the problem solving approach is the best way to solve problems.

In order to manage the complexity of the human survival problem it needs to be broken down into manageable parts. And the manageable parts need to be specific, doable actions. So, the basic format of a solution defined here is "a list of doable actions that need to be performed to solve a specific problem." The basic format of the solution to the human survival problem is "a list of doable actions that need to be performed to solve the problem of human survival of the universe."

In addition to breaking down the solution to the human survival problem into doable actions, the problem solving approach characterized here also focuses on *maximizing problem solving skill over time* as necessary to address the complexity of the human survival problem.

A focus on maximizing problem solving skill over time is necessary for the following reasons:

1) *maximum clarity of problem identification* – maximum problem solving skill over time includes the skill of clearly identifying the human survival problems;

2) *maximum problem solving performance* – maximum problem solving skill over time includes the skill of maximizing performance on the doable actions;

3) *optimal emotional experience* – maximum problem solving skill over time includes the skill of optimizing emotional experience (happiness) during the performance of the doable actions;

4) *maximum performance improvement over time* – maximum problem solving skill over time includes a built-in feedback mechanism which facilitates critical feedback on problem solving performance. This feedback is then used to correct mistakes, adapt to change, deal with unknowns, maintain stability, and improve performance over time;

5) *it's the truth* – we can be certain that we are going to need to maximize our problem solving skill over time due to the maximum complexity of the human survival problem imposed by the universe.

Point #3 The best way to find the correct solution to the human survival problem is by means of the scientific method.

Why is the scientific method the best way to find the correct solution? The scientific method is the best method because it leads to results that are:

a) *accurate* - science focuses on the definition and use of accurate terms, which facilitates problem solving by means of a clear and accurate definition of the problem and solution;

b) *reliable* – once proven, scientific results can be relied upon over time;

c) *objective* – scientific results are objective and avoid subjectivity and bias;

d) *testable* – scientific results are testable so that can be continuously tested, re-evaluated, improved and corrected where necessary.

In short, the scientific method is the best way to identify the correct solution to a problem, with the correct solution being in the format of "the correct list of actions." This way we will know the correct actions to take before we take them, and will not waste time and energy on the wrong actions.

The Three Hypotheses of the Ultimate World Context

So that the three points of the Ultimate World Context can be made accurate, reliable, objective and testable, they are hereby transformed into the three hypotheses of the Ultimate World Context. Note that you will need to read Chapter 2 to understand the science that underlies this transformation. Also note that the prefix "HC" is used to designate these three hypotheses as context hypotheses.

Hypothesis ID# = [HC1]
HC1 Establishing and maintaining the human survival issue as the most important issue is a necessary action because it is common sense to do so, and because human extinction would be the most catastrophic event imaginable to humans.

Hypothesis ID# = [HC2]
HC2 Establishing and maintaining a problem solving approach to the human survival issue based on maximum problem solving skill over time is a necessary action because it resolves the maximum complexity of the human survival problem imposed by the universe.

Hypothesis ID# = [HC3]
HC3 Establishing and maintaining a scientific solution to
the human survival problem is a necessary action because
a scientific solution is accurate, reliable, objective and
testable.

2

THE SCIENCE OF
THE ULTIMATE WORLD

The science of the Ultimate World is a big issue because of the need to identify the correct actions before performing any actions. A *correct* action is one that actually solves the problem. Knowing the correct actions before performing any actions makes it much easier to solve the problem. All you have to do is perform the correct action identified by the science. There is no wasted time or energy on trial and error.

The science of the Ultimate World consists of four main sections:

1) the UW scientific problem;
2) the UW scientific method;
3) the new school of UW science;
4) the UW scientific solution.

The UW Scientific Problem

All science begins with a scientific problem, or a question, where the problem is to answer the question.

As given in the introduction to this book, the UW problem is defined as "survive the universe using the minimum resources." Addressing the problem scientifically involves applying the scientific method. The Basic Scientific Method is explained with examples in Appendix A1, refer to it as necessary. The UW scientific method, which is derived directly from the Basic Scientific Method, is described in detail in the next section of this chapter.

In defining the UW scientific problem here, we will apply only the first step of the UW scientific method. The first step is officially called the *characterizations*, and involves defining the UW units of analysis and their measurements. The UW context, which was defined in chapter 1, provides the basis for the UW units of analysis, and their measurements.

In human life, the unit of analysis is the individual person. To be consistent with the UW context, we will take a problem solving approach to the definition of the person. So the individual person will be characterized as an Ultimate Person (UP), where a UP is defined as a person who maximizes problem solving skill over time. Maximizing problem solving skill over time is necessary to resolve the maximum complexity of the problem of surviving the universe using minimum resources, so the goal is to maximize the number of UPs.

People require resources to survive such as food, water, oxygen, medicine, and shelter. Taking a problem solving approach to acquiring human life resources involves characterizing the unit of resource acquisition as *the action required to obtain the resource*, and then characterizing these actions as *problem solving actions* (PSAs). Since life resources are limited, and PSAs have costs -- similar to labor costs in a business -- the goal is to minimize the number of PSAs.

Measuring the units in the UW problem involves the application of efficiency theory where efficiency is defined as the ratio of output to input and is given in the following formula:

$$\text{Efficiency} = \frac{\text{Output}}{\text{Input}}$$

Higher efficiency is achieved by increasing output and/or decreasing input. See Appendix A4 for a more detailed explanation and examples of efficiency theory. Efficiency theory is appropriate in this case because there are two primary units involved – one needs to be maximized (ultimate people), and one needs to be minimized (problem solving actions).

Adapting efficiency theory to the UW problem leads to the following formula:

$$\text{UW Efficiency} = \frac{\text{Ultimate People}}{\text{Problem Solving Actions}}$$

where the output of the UW scientific problem is ultimate people, and the input is problem solving actions. UW efficiency is the ratio of Ultimate People to Problem Solving Actions.

In order to maximize UW Efficiency, we must maximize the number of Ultimate People and minimize the number of Problem Solving Actions. So the formula for Maximum UW Efficiency is:

Maximum UW Efficiency =

$$\frac{\text{Maximum Number of Ultimate People}}{\text{Minimum Number of Problem Solving Actions}}$$

or in short form,

$$\text{Maximum UW Efficiency} = \frac{\text{UP}_{\text{MAX}}}{\text{PSA}_{\text{MIN}}}$$

This formula for Maximum UW Efficiency serves as the definition of the UW scientific problem.

The UW Scientific Method

The scientific method is a collection of techniques for investigating phenomena, acquiring new knowledge, or correcting and integrating previous knowledge. Although there are different ways of outlining the basic method used for scientific inquiry, the scientific community generally agrees on the following classification of method elements:

1) *Characterizations* – definitions, observations and measurements of the subject of inquiry
2) *Hypotheses* – theoretical explanations of the characterizations
3) *Predictions* – logical deduction from the hypotheses
4) *Experiments* – tests of all of the above.

The Basic Scientific Method is explained further with examples in Appendix A1. The UW Scientific Method is derived directly from this four step iterative process, adapted to the UW context and the UW scientific problem.

THE UW SCIENTIFIC METHOD

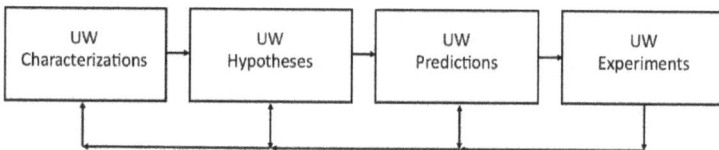

The UW scientific method diagram illustrates the four steps and the iterative nature of cycling through the four steps.

Remember that the UW scientific problem is:

$$\text{Maximum UW Efficiency} = \frac{UP_{MAX}}{PSA_{MIN}}$$

The UW scientific method addresses the "PSA_{MIN}" component (i.e. the UW input) of the UW scientific problem. Minimizing problem solving actions is characterized by efficiency by means of a focus on *necessity*. The goal of the UW scientific method, therefore, is to identify the actions that are *necessary* to maximize the number of UPs (i.e. the UW output). In essence, the UW scientific method is an action identification method.

The Format of the UW Scientific Method

The UW scientific method uses a format that is structured in terms of a data structure based on individual data fields. Data fields are the basic unit of information that can be entered into a computer.

The PSA Data Fields

The overall purpose of the PSA data fields is to provide necessary and detailed problem solving information. By knowing the details about each problem and solution, the resulting PSA will be accurate and reliable, and should lead to a successful solution.

The basic PSA data fields used to define PSAs are listed below. There are eleven basic PSA data fields:

1) *PSA ID#* – PSA ID# is a numerical, quantitative identity for each PSA. A numerical identity is necessary to give each PSA a unique identity.

2) *PSA name* – PSA name is a qualitative identity for each PSA. A qualitative identity is necessary to give each PSA properties

that can be shared with other PSAs. These PSA properties are implemented as other PSA data fields.

3) *Problem ID#* – Problem ID# is a quantitative identity for each problem. A quantitative identity is necessary to give each problem a unique identity. All problems stem from the UW scientific problem. Problems serve as the goals of the PSAs.

4) *Problem name* – Problem name is a qualitative identity for each problem. A qualitative identity is necessary to give each problem properties that can be shared with other problems.

5) *Action Name* – Action name is a qualitative identity for each action. A qualitative identity for each action is necessary to give each action properties that can be shared with other actions. Actions are necessary because all solutions are in the form of a list of actions. All action names are action words that when performed, solve the problems.

6) *Reason for Necessity* – Reasons for necessity provide the reasoning for why the PSA is necessary. Reasons for necessity ensure that the overall number of PSAs is minimized according to the UW scientific problem. They also add the dimension of relevance to the human survival problem.

7) *Unit of Analysis* – There are only two units of analysis within UW science: the Ultimate World (UW), and the Ultimate Person (UP). Units of analysis are necessary for the UW science to be quantified and measured. Note that there is only one UW obviously, but classifying it as a unit of analysis is necessary to distinguish it from individual UPs.

8) *Success Measure* – A success measure is either a quantitative or qualitative measure for the PSA problem. It is the entity used to determine whether problem has been solved or not.

9) *Time Deadline* – A time deadline is a specific time, defined as a specific date and time, for the completion of the PSA. A time deadline data field is necessary to encourage efficient completion of the PSAs.

10) *Supplemental Definitions* – Supplemental definitions can be used to provide clarifications to the PSA where necessary.

11) *Supplemental Reasoning* – Supplemental reasoning is additional reasons to strengthen the reason for necessity specified above.

Data Fields and Format

Now we address how these data fields, *along with their appropriate data format*, fit into the four steps of the UW scientific method. Similar to the basic scientific method, the UW scientific method has four primary steps:

1) UW Characterizations – UW characterizations serve as the definitions and measurements within UW Theory.

Characterization data fields: all eleven of the basic PSA data fields are included in the characterizations for each PSA. *Note that there is a supplemental data field for Characterization ID#, so that each characterization can be uniquely identified.*

Characterization format:

Characterization ID# = []
PSA name = []
PSA ID# = []
Problem name = []
Problem ID# = []
Action name = []
Reason for necessity = []
Unit of analysis = []

Time deadline = []
Success measure = []
Supplemental definitions = []
Supplemental reasoning = []

2) UW Hypotheses – UW hypotheses are the theoretical explanations of the PSA data fields. The basic theoretical explanation is
that a certain PSA is necessary because of its reason for necessity.
The list of UW hypotheses is the actual UW theory. It is summarized in Chapter 4.

Hypothesis data fields: there are only two data fields for each hypothesis – PSA name and reason for necessity. *Note that there is
a supplemental data field for Hypothesis ID#, so that each hypothesis can be uniquely identified.*

Hypothesis format:

Hypothesis ID# = [Hypothesis ID#]
[PSA name] is a necessary action because [Reason for necessity]

3) UW Predictions – UW predictions are the logical deductions
from the UW hypotheses. The basic logical deduction is that a
certain PSA will be performed in the future because it is necessary for human survival. The list of UW predictions are actual
predictions for the future. It is summarized in Chapter 5.

Prediction data fields: there are only two data fields for each prediction – problem name and action name. *Note that there is a
supplemental data field for Prediction ID#, so that each prediction can be uniquely identified.*
Prediction format:

Prediction ID# = [Prediction ID#]
[Problem Name] will be [Action Name] because it is necessary
for human survival.

4) UW Experiments – UW experiments are tests of all of the above. They can be tests on anything, including but not limited to characterizations, hypotheses, predictions or experiments. However, the majority of experiments are tests on hypotheses. This is because the hypotheses are specific explanations for why a PSA is necessary. Chapter 6 is devoted to UW experiments.

Experiment data fields: the majority of experiments are in the same format as a hypothesis and therefore have only two data fields: PSA name, and reason for necessity. *Note that there is a supplemental data field for Experiment ID# so that each experiment can be uniquely identified. And there is a supplemental data field for experiment type to identify the two types of experiments: ADD PSA and DELETE PSA.*

Experiment format:

There are two different formats of UW experiments, one for each type: ADD PSA and DELETE PSA.

ADD PSA – Standard hypothesis format: [PSA name] is a necessary action because [Reason for necessity]

DELETE PSA – Standard hypothesis format except change "is a necessary action" to "is not a necessary action" because of "reason for not-necessity": [PSA name] is not a necessary action because [Reason for not-necessity]

Note that an experiment designed to change an existing hypotheses involves two steps. The first step is to perform a DELETE hypothesis experiment. The second step is to perform an ADD hypothesis experiment to update the hypothesis with the new information.

The New School of Ultimate World Science

The vast majority of science is descriptive and describes "the way things are." The Ultimate World science is different and is *necessitive*, and defines "the way things need to be." The word *necessitive* is a new term, defined here for the first time, that makes for a convenient comparison to the conventional descriptive science.

The validity of a descriptive theory is addressed by means of empirical studies or mathematical analysis. The validity of a *necessitive* theory is addressed by means of verifying the necessity of an action to solve a problem. In the Ultimate World, the overall goal is human survival of the universe, so validity in Ultimate World science is addressed by means of verifying the necessity of an action for human survival of the universe. In short, validity in Ultimate World science involves the simple statement – "is it really do or die" for the world.

So the new school of Ultimate World science is the science of "do or die" for the world. The UW scientific method puts this new school of science into practice.

Note that necessitive science is not a replacement for descriptive science. It integrates descriptive science into it and focuses everything on solutions to human problems.

An effective way to compare descriptive science with necessitive science is to compare the format of their hypotheses. Descriptive hypotheses typically address causation and are in the following format "A causes B." A basic example of a descriptive hypothesis is "smoking causes lung cancer." There is plenty of empirical data that proves this hypothesis. So we can speak with credibility by saying "smoking causes lung cancer" and that is just the way things are.

The format of a necessitive hypotheses is "A is a necessary action because B" where A is an action, and B is a reason why A is a necessary action. An example of a necessitive hypothesis is "stopping people from smoking is a necessary action because smoking causes lung cancer."

The next section of this chapter – *The UW Scientific Solution* – provides numerous examples of necessitive hypotheses. This collection of necessitive hypotheses is the actual "Ultimate World Theory" that is specified in the introduction of this book. Chapter 4 provides a summary of the UW hypotheses in both list and diagram form.

Distinct Characteristics of The New School of Necessitive Science

Necessitive knowledge, which defines "the way things need to be," is completely distinct from descriptive knowledge, which describes "the way things are." Necessitive knowledge does share some characteristics with procedural knowledge, however, which describes how best to perform a task.

Both necessitive knowledge and procedural knowledge are similar in that they are both task dependent, and are therefore more specific and less general than descriptive knowledge. For example, the specific knowledge one uses to solve specific problems (procedural) differs from the general knowledge one has about problem solving (descriptive) because procedural knowledge is formed by defining and performing specific actions to solve a specific problem.

They key difference between necessitive knowledge and procedural knowledge is *relevance*. Necessitive knowledge pertains only to the top level problem of human survival. All sub-problems addressed by necessitive knowledge are derived directly from the human survival problem. The sub-problems relate directly to the top-level problem by means of their reasons for necessity. Remember that all actions identified in necessitive knowledge include a data field entitled "reason for necessity."

By contrast, procedural knowledge is knowledge about how to solve any problem, whether it is relevant to the super-problem of human survival or not. For example, procedural knowledge can be knowledge about how to solve Rubik's cube, which is not directly relevant to human survival. So the knowledge of solving Rubik's cube is procedural, but not necessitive.

And necessitive knowledge is also distinct from a "necessary condition" which is used in implicating statements in formal logic. Necessary conditions are typically used along with sufficient conditions to determine the truth about a statement. For example, taking a bus to work is a *sufficient condition* for arriving to work. It is not a *necessary condition* for arriving to work because there are other ways to get to work (car, carpool, walking, etc.). So, the statement of "taking a bus to work is a necessary condition to arrive at work" is a false statement. By contrast, the statement of "taking a bus to work is a sufficient condition to arrive at work," is a true statement.

Necessitive knowledge defines the bus travel problem as: "taking a bus to work is necessary *because* it is the only means for a specific person to get to work." This specific person has no car, no carpool, and the distance to work is too far to walk. Furthermore, the bus travel relates to survival because if this specific person does not arrive at work, then this person will not get paid, and will not be able to buy life necessities such as food, water and shelter. Therefore, taking a bus to work for this specific person is "do or die" which is the key distinction of necessitive knowledge. By contrast, in formal logic most necessary conditions are not do or die for the world because they are not directly relevant to the human survival problem. For example, the statement of "lightning is a necessary condition for thunder" is true because thunder never occurs without lightning. However, lightning is not a do or die occurrence for human survival.

In summary, necessitive knowledge is new and distinct from any other school of knowledge in terms of its relevance to the super problem of human survival. It answers the question of "is this action really do or die for the world, or not?"

Representing Necessitive Knowledge in the Computer

Artificial intelligence is a branch of computer science that deals with representing human knowledge in a computer, and then applying this computer based representation to solve human problems. See Appendix A5 for more detail on artificial intelligence theory. A sub-field of artificial intelligence, known as *Expert Systems,* will play a central role in UW Theory. Expert Systems mimic a human expert, such as a medical doctor, by using expert knowledge in the form of IF-THEN rules. IF-THEN rules are a knowledge format that is both: a) intuitive so that human experts (who are not necessarily computer science experts) can understand and apply it; and b) can be easily coded by computer programmers. The specific nature of the use of expert systems in UW Theory will be defined in the next section, entitled The UW Scientific Solution.

Descriptive IF-THEN rules state that IF "this" THEN "that is the way things are." An example of a descriptive IF-THEN rule is IF "one needs transportation to work" THEN "taking a bus is an option to get to work."

Necessitive IF-THEN rules are actually IF-THEN-BE-CAUSE rules. The IF-THEN-BECAUSE format is a new innovation in AI. In particular, the BECAUSE element is actually - BECAUSE- NECESSARY- FOR- HUMAN- SURVIVAL since it is implemented in the context of the new necessitive science.

An example of an IF-THEN- BECAUSE- NECESSARY- FOR- HUMAN- SURVIVAL rule is IF "one needs transportation to work" THEN "taking the bus is necessary" BECAUSE- NECESSARY- FOR- HUMAN- SURVIVAL "taking the bus is the only option to get work." Taking the bus to work is not only necessary but necessary for survival, because one needs to get to work to get a paycheck to buy life resources such as food and shelter.

Over time, new AI techniques will be implemented as necessitive knowledge. At the time of this publication, an AI technique called *Machine Learning* is very popular. Machine Learning involves the use of mathematical statistics and algorithms in computer software that allows the computer to learn *without being explicitly programmed by a human.* Search engines such as Google, and intelligent voice assistants such as Amazon's Alexa are based on machine learning.

However, machine learning is not suitable for the direct implementation of necessitive knowledge because it excludes human programming by definition. There is a major safety issue involved in allowing computers to determine human survival knowledge without human programming. Everyone's fear that machines will gain control over humans could be realized. Machine learning (i.e. machine programming) must therefore be secondary to human programming for implementation of necessitive knowledge.

By contrast, expert systems require *explicit* programming from a human expert and facilitate this human programming into a human made knowledge base. Expert systems is a human-programmed AI technique and is therefore suitable for implementation of necessitive knowledge.

Necessitive Knowledge and the Theory of Everything

The Theory of Everything is a descriptive theory of physics that fully explains and integrates all physical aspects of the universe. Current efforts to find the Theory of Everything are focused on integrating the physics of the very big (General Relativity) and the very small (Quantum Mechanics). However, since General Relativity and Quantum Mechanics are fundamentally incompatible theories, the search for the Theory of Everything has proven to be extremely difficult.

Necessitive science makes important contributions to the Theory of Everything and it also leads the way to finding the "Theory of Everything Relevant." The Theory of Everything Relevant is a theory that defines the actions that are relevant to human survival of the universe (i.e. the actions that are do or die for the world). UW Theory is this Theory of Everything Relevant.

Since there are limited resources available to search for the descriptive Theory of Everything and since the necessitive UW Theory directly addresses the efficient use of resources, priority should be given to the development of the Theory of Everything Relevant (i.e. UW Theory). Moreover, UW Theory directly addresses the human survival problem in a practical manner. If the human species does not survive, the Theory of Everything is pointless.

The Theory of Everything is actually dependent on UW Theory for the following two reasons at least:

1) the Theory of Everything is dependent on the Basic Scientific Method and the Basic Scientific Method itself is a form of necessitive knowledge (see UW Hypothesis HC3, page 14 of this book); and

2) the Theory of Everything needs improvement from its current state, and UW Theory facilitates the necessary improvement over time.

IMPORTANT NOTE: the next section, entitled The UW Scientific Solution, is a long section (33 pages) based on the new format of The UW Scientific Method.

The UW Scientific Solution

Remember, the UW scientific problem is defined as:

$$\text{Maximum UW Efficiency} = \frac{UP_{MAX}}{PSA_{MIN}}$$

with the lower denominator PSA_{MIN} being directly addressed by the UW scientific method.

The UW scientific solution directly addresses the upper numerator of the UW scientific problem UP_{MAX}. This solution is developed by using the UW scientific method to define the necessary actions in the form of PSA_{MIN}, to solve the problem in the form of UP_{MAX}.

This solution is organized by levels in a hierarchical structure in a top down fashion. Each level contains the UW characterizations and the UW hypotheses. The UW predictions and UW experiments are given in chapters 5 and 6 respectively.

The Top Level Scientific Solution

The top level solution is defined by using the UW scientific method to formulate the Top Level characterizations and the Top Level hypothesis. The Top Level hypothesis then serves as the Top Level scientific solution. Here is the terminology:

Top Level Problem = UP_{MAX}

Top Level Characterizations

Characterization ID# = [C1.0]
PSA ID# = [PSA 1.0]
PSA name = [Establish and maintain UP_{MAX}]
Problem ID# = [Problem 1.0]
Problem name [UP_{MAX}]

Action name = [Establish and maintain]
Reason for necessity = [Because of the maximum problem complexity of the human survival problem, which requires maximum problem solving skill over time to resolve this maximum problem complexity]
Unit of analysis = [Ultimate World (UW)]
Time deadline = [No time deadline (i.e. infinity)]
Success measure = [Maximum number of UPs]
Supplemental definitions = [1) maximum problem complexity = survive the universe using minimum resources, 2) maximum problem solving skill over time = UP_{MAX}, 3) universe = all safe locations and all time, 4) UW = Worldwide group of UPs. 5) UP = person who maximizes problem solving skill over time].
Supplemental reasons for necessity = [1) UP_{MAX} is necessary for maximum clarity of problem identification, 2) UP_{MAX} is necessary for maximum problem solving performance, 3) UP_{MAX} is necessary for maximum individual and world happiness, 4) UP_{MAX} is necessary for maximum performance improvement over time, 5) UP_{MAX} can be stated with certainty.

Top Level Hypothesis (i.e. The Supreme Hypothesis)

Hypothesis ID# = [H1.0]
H1.0 Establishing and maintaining UP_{MAX} is a necessary action because of the maximum problem complexity of the human survival problem, which requires maximum problem solving skill over time to resolve this maximum problem complexity.

Note – the short form of The Supreme Hypothesis is:

$$UW = UP_{MAX}$$

The Level 2 Scientific Solution

The Level 2 solution is defined by first sub-dividing the Level 1 problem into the Level 2 sub-problems. Then the UW

scientific method is used to formulate the Level 2 characterizations and Level 2 hypotheses. The Level 2 hypotheses serve as
the Level 2 scientific solution. Here are the steps involved:

> Step 1 – Problem 1.0 UP$_{MAX}$ is sub-divided into the fol-
> lowing sub-problems: Problem 2.1 UPs for all safe loca-
> tions in the universe; Problem 2.2 maximum group UP
> problem solving performance; and Problem 2.3 UPs for
> all time.
> Step 2 – The Level 2 characterizations and hypotheses are
> defined as follows:

Level 2 Characterizations

Characterization ID# = [C2.1]
PSA ID# = [PSA 2.1]
PSA name = [Establish and maintain UPs for all safe locations in
the universe]
Problem ID# = [Problem 2.1]
Problem name = [UPs for all safe locations in the universe]
Action name = [Establish and maintain]
Reason for necessity = [Because locations in the universe (in-
cluding planet earth) are not permanently safe for human habita-
tion]
Unit of analysis = [UW]
Time deadline = [No time deadline (i.e. infinity)]
Success measure = [All safe locations in the universe]
Supplemental definitions = [Safe locations are those locations
that can be made safe for human habitation]

Characterization ID# = [C2.2]
PSA ID# = [PSA 2.2]
PSA name = [Establish and maintain maximum group UP prob-
lem solving performance]
Problem ID# = [Problem 2.2]
Problem name = [Maximum group UP problem solving perfor-
mance]

Action name = [Establish and maintain]
Reason for necessity = [Because maximum group UP problem solving performance is required for solving complex survival problems over time]
Unit of analysis = [UW]
Time deadline = [No time deadline (i.e. infinity)]
Success measure = [All group members are certified UPs]
Supplemental definitions = [Maximum group UP problem solving performance = all group members are certified UPs]

Characterization ID# = [C2.3]
PSA ID# = [PSA 2.3]
PSA name = [Establish and maintain UPs for all time]
Problem ID# = [Problem 2.3]
Problem name [UPs for all time]
Action name = [Establish and maintain]
Reason for necessity = [Because individual UPs do not have permanent lifetimes]
Unit of analysis = [UW]
Time deadline = [No time deadline (i.e. infinity)]
Success measure = [UPs for all time (i.e. infinity)]

Level 2 Hypotheses

Hypothesis ID# = [H2.1]
H2.1 Establishing and maintaining UPs for all safe locations is a necessary action because locations in the universe (including planet earth) are not permanently safe for human habitation.

Hypothesis ID# = [H2.2]
H2.2 Establishing and maintaining maximum group UP problem solving performance is a necessary action because maximum group UP problem solving performance is required for solving complex survival problems over time.

Hypothesis ID# = [H2.3]

H2.3 Establishing and maintaining UPs for all time is a necessary action because individual UPs do not have permanent lifetimes.

The Level 3 Scientific Solution

The Level 3 solution is defined by first sub-dividing the Level 2 problems into the Level 3 sub-problems. Then the UW scientific method is used to formulate the Level 3 characterizations and Level 3 hypotheses. The Level 3 hypotheses serve as the Level 3 scientific solution. Here are the steps involved:

Step 1 – Problem 2.1 UPs for all safe locations in the universe is sub-divided into Problem 3.1 the Human Survival Problem Solver. Problem 2.2 maximum group UP problem solving performance is sub-divided into Problem 3.2 the Ultimate World. Problem 2.3 is sub-divided into Problem 3.3 the control theory framework.

Step 2 – The Level 3 characterizations and hypotheses are defined as follows:

Level 3 Characterizations

Characterization ID# = [C3.1]
PSA ID# = [PSA 3.1]
PSA name = [Establish and maintain HSPS]
Problem ID# = [Problem 3.1]
Problem name [Human Survival Problem Solver (HSPS)]
Action name = [Establish and maintain]
Reason for necessity = [Because a world-wide computer based solutions manager is necessary to manage all human survival problems in all safe locations in the universe and all time]
Unit of analysis = [Ultimate World (UW)]
Time deadline = [No time deadline (i.e. infinity)]
Success measure = [Solutions for all problems in all safe locations in the universe and all time]

Supplemental definitions = [HSPS = a world-wide computer based solutions manager for managing all human survival problems in all safe locations in the universe and all time. The HSPS is also known as the future of the internet]

Characterization ID# = [C3.2]
PSA ID# = [PSA 3.2]
PSA name = [Establish and maintain the UW]
Problem ID# = [Problem 3.2]
Problem name [Ultimate World (UW)]
Action name = [Establish and maintain]
Reason for necessity = [Because a world-wide group of UPs that work together as a team is necessary to maximize group problem solving skill over time]
Unit of analysis = [Ultimate World (UW)]
Time deadline = [No time deadline (i.e. infinity)]
Success measure = [All group members are certified UPs]
Supplemental definitions = [UW = world-wide team of UPs that work together as a team to maximize group problem solving skill over time]

Characterization ID# = [C3.3]
PSA ID# = [PSA 3.3]
PSA name = [Establish and maintain CTF]
Problem ID# = [Problem 3.3]
Problem name [Control theory framework for integrating HSPS and UW]
Action name = [Establish and maintain]
Reason for necessity = [Because control theory facilitates maximum use of feedback between HSPS and UW to correct mistakes, adapt to change, deal with unknowns, maintain UW stability and maximize performance improvement over time]
Unit of analysis = [Ultimate World (UW)]
Time deadline = [No time deadline (i.e. infinity)]

Success measure = [Maximum use of feedback between HSPS and UW to correct mistakes, adapt to change, deal with unknowns, maintain UW stability and maximize problem solving performance over time.]

Supplemental definitions = [CTF = Control Theory Framework for integration of HSPS and UW. Control Theory Framework has five primary elements: controller, reference, system input, system output, and system]

Level 3 Hypotheses

Hypothesis ID# = [H3.1]

H3.1 Establishing and maintaining the Human Survival Problem Solver is a necessary action because a world-wide computer based solutions manager is necessary to manage all human survival problems in all safe locations in the universe and all time.

Hypothesis ID# = [H3.2]

H3.2 Establishing and maintaining the Ultimate World is a necessary action because a world-wide group of UPs that work together as a team is necessary to maximize group problem solving skill over time.

Hypothesis ID# = [H3.3]

H3.3 Establishing and maintaining a Control Theory Framework for integrating HSPS and UW is a necessary action because control theory facilitates maximum use of feedback between HSPS and UW to correct mistakes, adapt to change, deal with unknowns, maintain UW stability and maximize performance improvement over time.

CONTROL THEORY FRAMEWORK

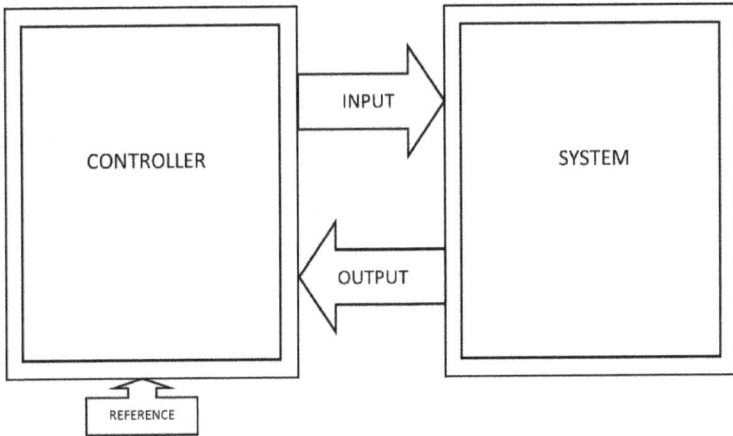

The control theory framework diagram illustrates the framework of the five elements of a control system: the input, the output, the system, the controller, and the reference.

ULTIMATE WORLD THEORY

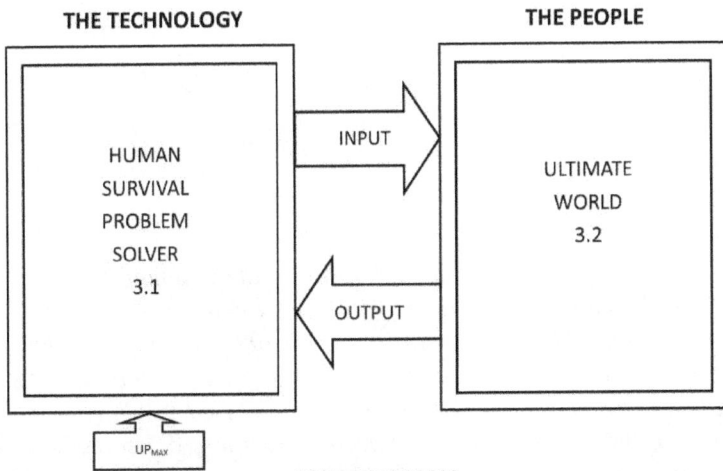

LEVEL 3 DIAGRAM

The Level 3 diagram illustrates how the Ultimate World (UW) and the Human Survival Problem Solver (HSPS) are integrated within the control theory framework. The UW (problem ID# 3.2) is the system and the HSPS (problem ID# 3.1) is the controller.

IMPORTANT NOTE. Starting with Level 4, the Ultimate World Solution (The People) is separated from the Human Survival Problem Solver Solution (The Technology). The people issues are separated from the technology issues so that the people issues can be given special attention. These people issues are addressed in Chapter 3 The Practice of the Ultimate World. Specifically, the UW People Solution begins on page 73. The UW Technology Solution continues below.

The UW Technology Scientific Solution

The UW Technology Solution is defined as the HSPS Level 4 scientific solution. The HSPS Level 4 solution is defined by first sub-dividing the Level 3 problems into the Level 4 sub-problems. Then the UW scientific method is used to formulate the Level 4 characterizations and Level 4 hypotheses. The Level 4 hypotheses serve as the Level 4 scientific solution. Here are the steps involved:

Step 1 – Problem 3.1 The Human Survival Problem Solver is sub-divided into the following sub-problems: Problem HC4.1 controller within HSPS, and Problem HR4.1 reference within HSPS.

Step 2 – The Level 4 characterizations and hypotheses are defined as follows:

The HSPS Level 4 Characterizations

Characterization ID# = [CHC4.1]
PSA ID# = [PSA HC4.1]
PSA name = [Establish and maintain a controller in HSPS]
Problem ID# = [Problem HC4.1]
Problem name [Controller within HSPS]
Action name = [Establish and maintain]
Reason for necessity = [Because a controller is a necessary component of control theory]
Unit of analysis = [Ultimate World (UW)]
Time deadline = [No time deadline (i.e. infinity)]
Success measure = [Error free management of all UW solutions]
Supplemental definitions = [Controller = the primary purpose of a controller is to take the output of a system (i.e. the actual output), compare the output to the reference (i.e. the desired output), make corrections to this output if necessary, and then send new

input to a system. The HSPS controller has two primary elements: 1) HSPS expert System; and 2) HSPS application Set].

Characterization ID# = [CHR4.1]
PSA ID# = [PSA HR4.1]
PSA name = [Establish and maintain a reference within HSPS]
Problem ID# = [Problem HR4.1]
Problem name [Reference within HSPS]
Action name = [Establish and maintain]
Reason for necessity = [Because a reference is a necessary element of control theory]
Unit of analysis = [Ultimate World (UW)]
Time deadline = [No time deadline (i.e. infinity)]
Success measure = [UP_{MAX}]
Supplemental definitions = [Reference – the primary purpose of a reference is to serve as the desired output of a system]

The HSPS Level 4 Hypotheses

HSPS Hypotheses

Hypothesis ID# = [HHC4.1]
HHC4.1 Establishing and maintaining a controller within HSPS is a necessary action because a controller is a necessary element of control theory.

Hypothesis ID# = [HHR4.1]
HHR4.1 Establishing and maintaining a reference in the HSPS is a necessary action because a reference is a necessary element of control theory.

THE TECHNOLOGY

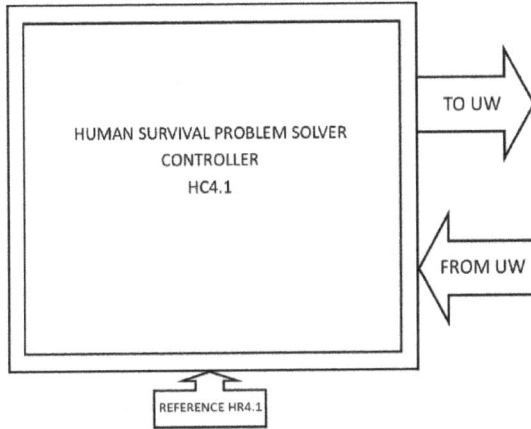

HSPS LEVEL 4 DIAGRAM

The HSPS Level 4 Diagram illustrates the two primary elements of the HSPS: the controller and the reference. Note that all HSPS elements have an "H" prefix on their problem IDs. For example, the HSPS controller ID# = HC4.1, and the HSPS reference ID# = HR4.1.

The HSPS Level 5 Scientific Solution

The HSPS Level 5 solution is defined by first sub-dividing the Level 4 problems into the Level 5 sub-problems. Then the UW scientific method is used to formulate the Level 5 characterizations and Level 5 hypotheses. The Level 5 hypotheses serve as the Level 5 scientific solution. Here are the steps involved:

Step 1 – Problem HC4.1 is sub-divided into the following sub-problems: Problem HC5.1 HSPS expert system and Problem HC5.2 HSPS application set. Problem HR4.1 is sub-divided into the following sub-problem: Problem HR5.1 UP$_{MAX}$ as the HSPS reference.

Step 2 – The Level 5 characterizations and hypotheses are defined as follows:

The HSPS Level 5 Characterizations

Controller Elements

Characterization ID# = [CHC5.1]
PSA ID# = [PSA HC5.1]
PSA name = [Establish and maintain a HSPS Expert System]
Problem ID# = [Problem HC5.1]
Problem name [HSPS Expert System]
Action name = [Establish and maintain]
Reason for necessity = [Because an expert system is necessary to manage the specialized sub-problems of UP$_{MAX}$ in a computer-based, safe, intelligent fashion]
Unit of analysis = [Ultimate World (UW)]
Time deadline = [No time deadline (i.e. infinity)]
Success measure = [Error free management of the specialized sub-problems of UP$_{MAX}$]
Supplemental definitions = 1. [Expert system – expert systems are intelligent computer systems that explicitly implement human intelligence in the form of IF-THEN rules]. 2. [An expert system will serve as the operating system of HSPS]

Characterization ID# = [CHC5.2]
PSA ID# = [PSA HC5.2]
PSA name = [Establish and maintain a HSPS application set]
Problem ID# = [Problem HC5.2]
Problem name [HSPS application set]
Action name = [Establish and maintain]
Reason for necessity = [Because an application set is necessary to identify and perform specific solutions to specific problem types within the human survival problem]
Unit of analysis = [Ultimate World (UW)]

Time deadline = [No time deadline (i.e. infinity)]
Success measure = [Error free performance of the applications]
Supplemental definitions = [Application – a specific solution, or set of solutions, to a specific problem type]

Reference Elements

Characterization ID# = [CHR5.1]
PSA ID# = [PSA HR5.1]
PSA name = [Establish and maintain UP_{MAX} as the reference]
Problem ID# = [Problem HR5.1]
Problem name [UP_{MAX} as the HSPS reference]
Action name = [Establish and maintain]
Reason for necessity = [Because UP_{MAX} is the desired output of the UW]
Unit of analysis = [Ultimate World (UW)]
Time deadline = [No time deadline (i.e. infinity)]
Success measure = [UP_{MAX}]
Supplemental definitions = [Reference = the desired output of a system]

The HSPS Level 5 Hypotheses

Controller Hypotheses

Hypothesis ID# = [HHC5.1]
HHC5.1 Establishing and maintaining a HSPS expert system is a necessary action because an expert system is necessary to manage the specialized sub-problems of UP_{MAX} in a computer-based, safe, intelligent fashion.

Hypothesis ID# = [HHC5.2]
HHC5.2 Establishing and maintaining a HSPS application set is a necessary action because an application set is necessary to identify and perform specific solutions to specific problem types within the human survival problem.

Reference Hypotheses

Hypothesis ID# = [HHR5.1]
HHR5.1 Establishing and maintaining UP_{MAX} as the HSPS reference is a necessary action because UP_{MAX} is the desired output of the UW.

THE TECHNOLOGY

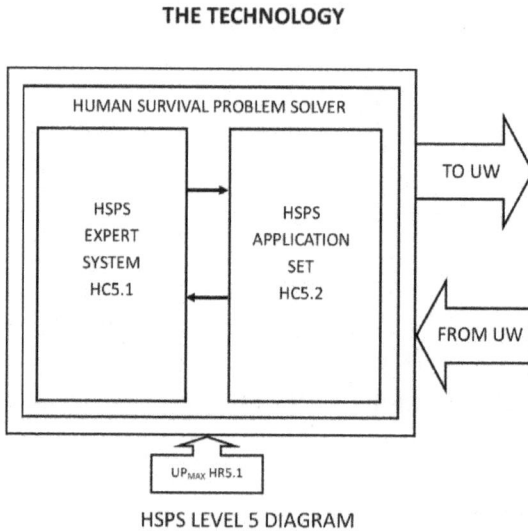

HSPS LEVEL 5 DIAGRAM

The HSPS Level 5 diagram illustrates the two primary elements of the HSPS controller: the HSPS expert system (problem ID# HC5.1) and the HSPS application set (problem ID# HC5.2). It also illustrates UP-$_{MAX}$ as the HSPS reference (problem ID# HR5.1).

The HSPS Level 6 Scientific Solution

The HSPS Level 6 solution is defined by first sub-dividing the Level 5 problems into the Level 6 sub-problems. Then the UW scientific method is used to formulate the Level 6 characterizations and Level 6 hypotheses. The Level 6 hypotheses serve as the Level 6 scientific solution. Here are the steps involved:

Step 1 – Problem HC5.1 HSPS expert system is sub-divided into the following sub-problems: Problem HES6.1 knowledge base; Problem HES6.2 HSPS inference engine; and Problem HES6.3 HSPS user interface. Problem HC5.2 HSPS application set is sub-divided into sub-problems: Problem HAS6.1 human survival problem identification application; Problem HAS6.2 space life economy application; Problem HAS6.3 UW education application; and Problem HAS6.4 safety awareness application.

Step 2 – The Level 6 characterizations and hypotheses are defined as follows:

The HSPS Level 6 Characterizations

HSPS Expert System Elements.

Characterization ID# = [CHES6.1]
PSA ID# = [PSA HES6.1]
PSA name = [Establish and maintain a HSPS Knowledge Base]
Problem ID# = [Problem HES 6.1]
Problem name [HSPS Knowledge Base]
Action name = [Establish and maintain]
Reason for necessity = [Because a knowledge base is a necessary element of an expert system]
Unit of analysis = [Ultimate World (UW)]
Time deadline = [No time deadline (i.e. infinity)]
Success measure = [Error free management of the knowledge base]
Supplemental definitions = [knowledge base = collection of knowledge represented in the computer in the form of IF-THEN rules]

Characterization ID# = [CHES6.2]
PSA ID# = [PSA HES6.2]

PSA name = [Establish and maintain a HSPS inference engine]
Problem ID# = [Problem HES6.2]
Problem name [HSPS inference engine]
Action name = [Establish and maintain]
Reason for necessity = [Because an inference engine is a necessary element of an expert system]
Unit of analysis = [Ultimate World (UW)]
Time deadline = [No time deadline (i.e. infinity)]
Success measure = [Error free management of the inference engine]
Supplemental definitions = [inference engine = software program for applying the knowledge base to the specific problems that are input through the user interface. It then reports the solutions to the user through the user interface. It also uses the user input to generate new knowledge and expand the knowledge base. It uses inference rules which can be also be in the form of IF-THEN rules.]

Characterization ID# = [CHES6.3]
PSA ID# = [PSA HES6.3]
PSA name = [Establish and maintain a HSPS user interface]
Problem ID# = [Problem HES6.3]
Problem name [HSPS user interface]
Action name = [Establish and maintain]
Reason for necessity = [Because a user interface is a necessary element of an expert system]
Unit of analysis = [Ultimate World (UW)]
Time deadline = [No time deadline (i.e. infinity)]
Success measure = [Error free management of the user interface]
Supplemental definitions = [user interface = computer based display to facilitate user input to the expert system. The user interface interacts directly with the inference engine. It reports three types of information to the user: 1) user input/output; 2) PSA List, 3) support]

HSPS Application Set Elements

Characterization ID# = [CHAS6.1]
PSA ID# = [PSA HAS6.1]
PSA name = [Establish and maintain a UW Theory Education application]
Problem ID# = [Problem HAS6.1]
Problem name [UW Theory education application]
Action name = [Establish and maintain]
Reason for necessity = [Because a UW Theory education application is necessary to maximize problem solving skill over time on the problem of educating the world on UW Theory and certifying everyone as UPs]
Unit of analysis = [Ultimate World (UW)]
Time deadline = [No time deadline (i.e. infinity)]
Success measure = [Error free performance of the UW Theory Education application]
Supplemental definitions = [UW Theory Education application – an online education course for educating the world on UW theory and to provide certification to everyone].

Characterization ID# = [CHAS6.2]
PSA ID# = [PSA HAS6.2]
PSA name = [Establish and maintain a Human Survival Problem Identification application]
Problem ID# = [Problem HAS6.2]
Problem name [Human Survival Problem Identification application]
Action name = [Establish and maintain]
Reason for necessity = [Because a human survival problem identification application is necessary to maximize problem solving skill over time on the problem of identifying human survival problems]
Unit of analysis = [Ultimate World (UW)]
Time deadline = [No time deadline (i.e. infinity)]
Success measure = [Error free performance of the human survival problem identification application]

Supplemental definitions = [Human Survival Problem Identification application – an application to maximize clarity of the human survival threats]

Characterization ID# = [CHAS6.3]
PSA ID# = [PSA HAS6.3]
PSA name = [Establish and maintain a Space Life Economy application]
Problem ID# = [Problem HAS6.3]
Problem name [Space Life Economy application]
Action name = [Establish and maintain]
Reason for necessity = [Because a space life economy application is necessary to maximize problem solving skill over time on the problem of managing a space life economy]
Unit of analysis = [Ultimate World (UW)]
Time deadline = [No time deadline (i.e. infinity)]
Success measure = [Error free performance of the space life economy application]
Supplemental definitions = [space life economy – a space-based economy similar to the current earth-based economy. Considers the current earth-based economy as a space-based economy that it is earth mode.]
Supplemental reasoning = [a space-based economy is necessary because life on earth is limited due to the natural warming of the sun]

Characterization ID# = [CHAS6.4]
PSA ID# = [PSA HAS6.4]
PSA name = [Establish and maintain a Safety Awareness application]
Problem ID# = [Problem HAS6.4]
Problem name [Safety Awareness application]
Action name = [Establish and maintain]
Reason for necessity = [Because a safety awareness application is necessary to maximize problem solving skill over time on the problem of safety awareness in all PSAs]
Unit of analysis = [Ultimate World (UW)]

Time deadline = [No time deadline (i.e. infinity)]
Success measure = [Error free performance of the safety awareness application]
Supplemental definitions = [Safety Awareness application – application to ensure safety awareness in all PSAs]

The HSPS Level 6 Hypotheses

HSPS Expert System Hypotheses

Hypothesis ID# = [HHES6.1]
HHES6.1 Establishing and maintaining a HSPS knowledge base
is a necessary action because a knowledge base is a necessary
element of an expert system.

Hypothesis ID# = [HHES6.2]
HHES6.2 Establishing and maintaining a HSPS inference engine
is a necessary action because an inference engine is a necessary
element of an expert system.

Hypothesis ID# = [HHES6.3]
HHES6.3 Establishing and maintaining a HSPS user interface is
a necessary action because a user interface is a necessary element
of an expert system.

HSPS Application Set Hypotheses

Hypothesis ID# = [HHAS6.1]
HHAS6.1 Establishing and maintaining a UW Theory education
application is a necessary action because a UW education application is necessary to maximize problem solving skill over time
on the problem of educating the world on UW Theory and certifying everyone as UPs.

Hypothesis ID# = [HHAS6.2]
HHAS6.2 Establishing and maintaining a Human Survival Problem Identification application is a necessary action because a human survival threat identification application is necessary to
maximize problem solving skill over time on the problem of
identifying human survival threats.

Hypothesis ID# = [HHAS6.3]
HHAS6.3 Establishing and maintaining a Space Life Economy
application is a necessary action because a space life economy
application is necessary to maximize problem solving skill over
time on the problem of managing a space life economy.

Hypothesis ID# = [HHAS6.4]
HHAS6.4 Establishing and maintaining a Safety Awareness application is a necessary action because a safety awareness application is necessary to maximize problem solving skill over time
on the problem of safety awareness in all PSAs.

THE TECHNOLOGY

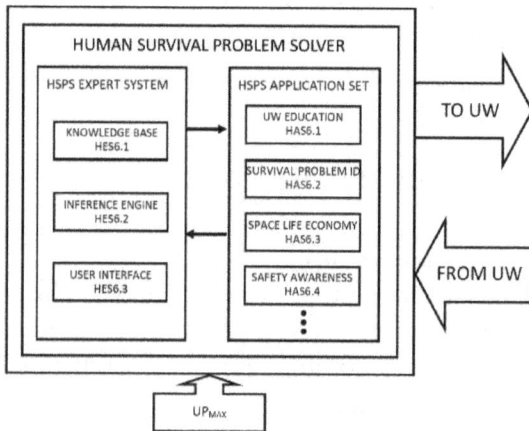

HSPS LEVEL 6 DIAGRAM

*The HSPS Level 6 diagram illustrates the detailed elements within the
HSPS expert system and the HSPS application Set. The HSPS expert*

system knowledge base problem ID# = HES6.1. The HSPS expert system inference engine problem ID# = HES6.2. The HSPS expert system user interface problem ID# = HES6.3. The HSPS UW Theory education application problem ID# = HAS6.1. The HSPS human survival problem ID application problem ID# = HAS6.2. The HSPS space life economy application problem ID# = HAS6.3. The HSPS safety awareness application problem ID# = HAS6.4.

The HSPS Level 7 Scientific Solution

The HSPS Level 7 solution is defined by first sub-dividing the Level 6 problems into the Level 7 sub-problems. Then the UW scientific method is used to formulate the Level 7 characterizations and Level 7 hypotheses. The Level 7 hypotheses serve as the Level 7 scientific solution. Here are the steps involved:

Step 1 – Problem HES6.1 HSPS knowledge base is subdivided into the following sub-problems: Problem HKB7.1 definitional knowledge base; and HKB7.2 performance knowledge base. Problem HES6.2 HSPS inference engine is sub-divided into the following sub-problems: Problem HIE7.1 definitional inference rule; and HIE7.2 performance inference rule. Problem HES6.3 user interface is sub-divided into the following sub-problems: Problem HUI7.1 user input/output; Problem HUI7.2 PSA list; and Problem HUI7.3 support. Problem HAS6.3 UW theory education application is sub-divided into Problem HASU7.1 UW Theory online course; and Problem HASU7.2 UW Skill online course

Step 2 – The Level 7 characterizations and hypotheses are defined as follows:

The HSPS Level 7 Characterizations

Knowledge Base Characterizations

Characterization ID# = [CHKB7.1]
PSA ID# = [PSA HKB7.1]
PSA name = [Establish and maintain a definitional knowledge base]
Problem ID# = [Problem HKB7.1]
Problem name [definitional knowledge base]
Action name = [Establish and maintain]
Reason for necessity = [Because a definitional knowledge base is necessary to manage PSA definitions in all HSPS applications]
Unit of analysis = [Ultimate World (UW)]
Time deadline = [No time deadline (i.e. infinity)]
Success measure = [Error free management of the definitional knowledge base]
Supplemental definitions = [definitional knowledge base – a knowledge base to manage PSA definitions for all HSPS applications]

Characterization ID# = [CHKB7.2]
PSA ID# = [PSA HKB7.2]
PSA name = [Establish and maintain a performance knowledge base]
Problem ID# = [Problem HKB7.2]
Problem name [performance knowledge base]
Action name = [Establish and maintain]
Reason for necessity = [Because a performance knowledge base is necessary to manage PSA performance knowledge in a way that maximizes user performance and user happiness for all HSPS applications]
Unit of analysis = [Ultimate World (UW)]
Time deadline = [No time deadline (i.e. infinity)]
Success measure = [Error free management of the performance knowledge base]
Supplemental definitions = [performance knowledge base – a knowledge base to maximize user performance and happiness]

Inference Engine Characterizations

Characterization ID# = [CHIE7.1]
PSA ID# = [PSA HIE7.1]
PSA name = [Establish and maintain a definitional inference rule]
Problem ID# = [Problem HIE7.1]
Problem name [definitional inference rule]
Action name = [Establish and maintain]
Reason for necessity = [Because a definitional inference rule is necessary to manage the interaction between the definitional knowledge base and users in a necessitive fashion]
Unit of analysis = [Ultimate World (UW)]
Time deadline = [No time deadline (i.e. infinity)]
Success measure = [Error free management of the definitional inference rule]
Supplemental definitions = [definitional inference rule – IF "definitional problem A" THEN "definitional solution B" BECAUSE- NECESSARY- FOR- SURVIVAL "reason for necessity C"]

Characterization ID# = [CHIE7.2]
PSA ID# = [PSA HIE7.2]
PSA name = [Establish and maintain a performance inference rule]
Problem ID# = [Problem HIE7.2]
Problem name [performance inference rule]
Action name = [Establish and maintain]
Reason for necessity = [Because a performance inference rule is necessary to manage the interaction between the performance knowledge base and users in a necessitive fashion]
Unit of analysis = [Ultimate World (UW)]
Time deadline = [No time deadline (i.e. infinity)]
Success measure = [Error free management of the performance inference rule]
Supplemental definitions = [performance inference rule – IF "performance problem A" THEN "performance solution B" BECAUSE- NECESSARY- FOR- SURVIVAL "reason for necessity C"]

User Interface Characterizations

Characterization ID# = [CHUI7.1]
PSA ID# = [PSA HUI7.1]
PSA name = [Establish and maintain an user input/output section of the user interface]
Problem ID# = [Problem HUI7.1]
Problem name [user input/output]
Action name = [Establish and maintain]
Reason for necessity = [Because a user input/output is necessary to facilitate user input and output from HSPS]
Unit of analysis = [Ultimate World (UW)]
Time deadline = [No time deadline (i.e. infinity)]
Success Measure = [Error free management of the user input/output]

Characterization ID# = [CHUI7.2]
PSA ID# = [PSA HUI7.2]
PSA name = [Establish and maintain a PSA List section of the user interface]
Problem ID# = [Problem HUI7.2]
Problem name [PSA List]
Action name = [Establish and maintain]
Reason for necessity = [Because a PSA List is necessary to manage the PSAs that the user will be performing]
Unit of analysis = [Ultimate World (UW)]
Time deadline = [No time deadline (i.e. infinity)]
Success measure = [Error free management of the PSA List]
Supplemental definitions = [PSA List – a list of PSAs that serve as the user's "to do list"]
Characterization ID# = [CHUI7.3]
PSA ID# = [PSA HUI7.3]
PSA name = [Establish and maintain a support section of the user interface]
Problem ID# = [Problem HUI7.3]
Problem name [support]
Action name = [Establish and maintain]

Reason for necessity = [Because support is necessary to assist users in maximizing performance on the PSA list]
Unit of analysis = [Ultimate World (UW)]
Time deadline = [No time deadline (i.e. infinity)]
Success Measure = [Error free management of the support section]
Supplemental definitions = [support–performance based support that implements the performance rules given in Chapter 3].

The HSPS Level 7 Hypotheses

Knowledge Base Hypotheses

Hypothesis ID# = [HHKB7.1]
HHKB7.1 Establishing and maintaining a definitional knowledge base is a necessary action because a definitional knowledge base is necessary to manage PSA definitions in all HSPS applications.

Hypothesis ID# = [HHKB7.2]
HHKB7.2 Establishing and maintaining a performance knowledge base is a necessary action because a performance knowledge base is necessary to manage user performance knowledge in a way that maximizes user performance and user happiness for all HSPS applications.

THE TECHNOLOGY

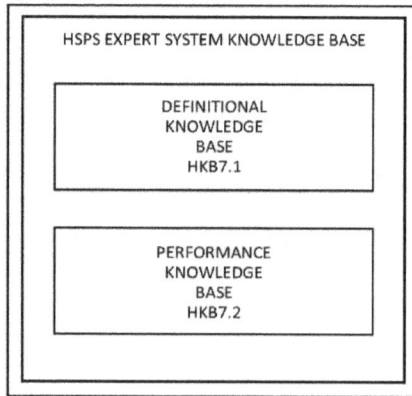

```
┌─────────────────────────────────────────┐
│ ┌─────────────────────────────────────┐ │
│ │  HSPS EXPERT SYSTEM KNOWLEDGE BASE   │ │
│ │                                     │ │
│ │    ┌───────────────────────────┐    │ │
│ │    │       DEFINITIONAL         │    │ │
│ │    │        KNOWLEDGE           │    │ │
│ │    │          BASE              │    │ │
│ │    │         HKB7.1             │    │ │
│ │    └───────────────────────────┘    │ │
│ │                                     │ │
│ │    ┌───────────────────────────┐    │ │
│ │    │       PERFORMANCE          │    │ │
│ │    │        KNOWLEDGE           │    │ │
│ │    │          BASE              │    │ │
│ │    │         HKB7.2             │    │ │
│ │    └───────────────────────────┘    │ │
│ │                                     │ │
│ └─────────────────────────────────────┘ │
└─────────────────────────────────────────┘
```

HSPS LEVEL 7 DIAGRAM 1

The HSPS Level 7 diagram 1 illustrates the two knowledge bases within the HSPS expert system knowledge base: the definitional knowledge base problem ID# = HKB7.1; and the performance knowledge base problem ID# = HKB7.2.

Inference Engine Hypotheses

Hypothesis ID# = [HHIE7.1]
HHIE7.1 Establishing and maintaining a definitional inference rule is a necessary action because a definitional inference rule is necessary to manage the interaction between the definitional knowledge bases and the users in a necessitive fashion.

Hypothesis ID# = [HHIE7.2]
HHIE7.2 Establishing and maintaining a performance inference rule is a necessary action because a performance inference rule is necessary to manage the interaction between the performance knowledge base and the users in a necessitive fashion.

THE TECHNOLOGY

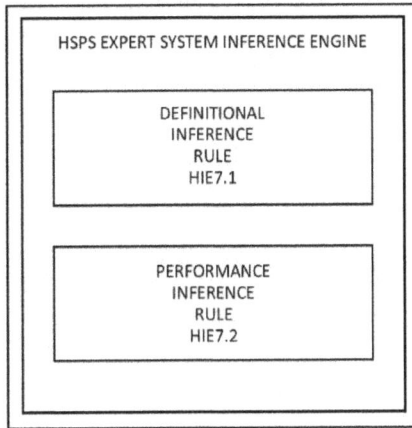

```
┌─────────────────────────────────────────────────┐
│  HSPS EXPERT SYSTEM INFERENCE ENGINE              │
│                                                   │
│      ┌───────────────────────────────────┐       │
│      │           DEFINITIONAL             │       │
│      │            INFERENCE               │       │
│      │              RULE                  │       │
│      │             HIE7.1                 │       │
│      └───────────────────────────────────┘       │
│                                                   │
│      ┌───────────────────────────────────┐       │
│      │           PERFORMANCE              │       │
│      │            INFERENCE               │       │
│      │              RULE                  │       │
│      │             HIE7.2                 │       │
│      └───────────────────────────────────┘       │
│                                                   │
└─────────────────────────────────────────────────┘
```

HSPS LEVEL 7 DIAGRAM 2

The HSPS Level 7 diagram 2 illustrates the two elements of the HSPS expert system inference engine: the definitional inference rule problem ID# = HIE7.1; and the performance inference rule problem ID# = HIE7.2.

User Interface Hypotheses

Hypothesis ID# = [HHUI7.1]
HHUI7.1 Establishing and maintaining a user input/output section of the user interface is a necessary action because a user input/output is necessary to facilitate user input and output from HSPS.

Hypothesis ID# = [HHUI7.2]

HHUI7.2 Establishing and maintaining a PSA List section of the user interface is a necessary action because a PSA List is necessary to manage the PSAs that the user will be performing.

Hypothesis ID# = [HHUI7.3]
HHUI7.3 Establishing and maintaining a support section of the user interface is a necessary action because support is necessary to assist users in maximizing performance on the PSA list.

THE TECHNOLOGY

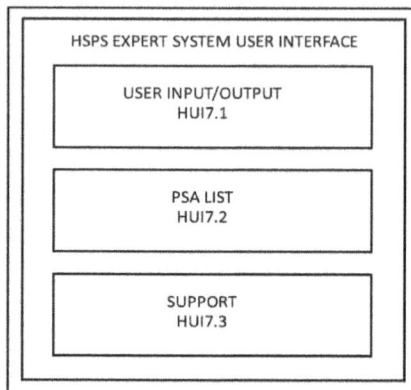

HSPS LEVEL 7 DIAGRAM 3

The HSPS Level 7 diagram 3 illustrates the three elements of the HSPS expert system user interface: the user input/output problem ID# = HUI7.1; the PSA list problem ID# = HUI7.2; and the support problem ID# = HUI7.3.

UW Theory Education Application Characterizations

UW Theory Online Course Characterization

Characterization ID# = [CHASU7.1]
PSA ID# = [PSA HASU7.1]
PSA name = [Establish and maintain a UW Theory online course]
Problem ID# = [Problem HASU7.1]

Problem name [UW Theory online course]
Action name = [Establish and maintain]
Reason for Necessity = [Because a UW Theory online course is a necessary to educate and certify UPs as experts on UW Theory]
Unit of analysis = [Ultimate World (UW)]
Time deadline = [No time deadline (i.e. infinity)]
Success measure = [Error free management of the UW Theory online course]
Supplemental definitions = [UW Theory online course – a online course on UW Theory that certifies UPs as experts on UW Theory]

UP Skill Online Course Characterization

Characterization ID# = [CHASU7.2]
PSA ID# = [PSA HASU7.2]
PSA name = [Establish and maintain a UP Skill online course]
Problem ID# = [Problem HAS7.2]
Problem name [UP Skill online course]
Action name = [Establish and maintain]
Reason for Necessity = [Because a UP Skill online course is a necessary to educate everyone in the world on UP Skill and certify everyone as UPs]
Unit of analysis = [Ultimate World (UW)]
Time deadline = [No time deadline (i.e. infinity)]
Success measure = [Error free management of the UP Skill online course]
Supplemental definitions = [UP Skill online course – a online course on UP Skill that also certifies everyone as UPs]

UW Theory Education Application Hypotheses

UW Theory Online Course Hypothesis

HHASU7.1 Establishing and maintaining a UW Theory online course is a necessary action because a UW Theory online course is necessary to educate and certify UPs as experts on UW Theory.

UP Skill Online Course Hypothesis

HHASU7.2 Establishing and maintaining a UP Skill online course is a necessary action because a UP Skill online course is necessary to educate everyone in the world on UP Skill and certify everyone as UPs.

THE TECHNOLOGY

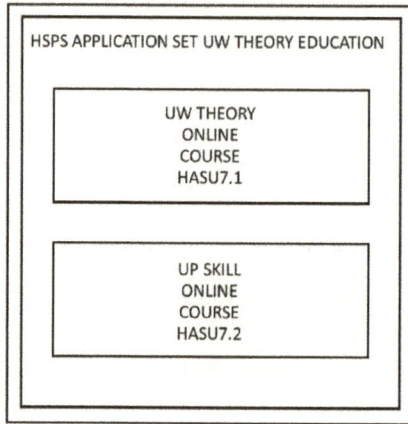

```
┌─────────────────────────────────────────┐
│                                         │
│ HSPS APPLICATION SET UW THEORY EDUCATION │
│                                         │
│   ┌───────────────────────────────┐     │
│   │         UW THEORY             │     │
│   │         ONLINE               │     │
│   │         COURSE               │     │
│   │         HASU7.1              │     │
│   └───────────────────────────────┘     │
│                                         │
│   ┌───────────────────────────────┐     │
│   │         UP SKILL             │     │
│   │         ONLINE               │     │
│   │         COURSE               │     │
│   │         HASU7.2              │     │
│   └───────────────────────────────┘     │
│                                         │
└─────────────────────────────────────────┘
```

HSPS LEVEL 7 DIAGRAM 4

The HSPS Level 7 diagram 4 illustrates the UW Theory online course problem ID# = HASU7.1, and the UP Skill online course problem ID# = HASU7.2.

Both of these online courses are now available, meaning that the implementation of Ultimate World Theory, and the construction of the Ultimate World is now underway.

3

THE PRACTICE OF
THE ULTIMATE WORLD

The practice of the Ultimate World is a big issue because of the need to produce results by solving actual problems. In UW theory, solutions are performed in *The People* section. This chapter focuses on the problem solving performance of *The People* section, and how to maximize this performance over time. This chapter also addresses the issue of individual and group happiness. The science of happiness shows us that action performance and happiness are directly linked. It shows us that maximum action performance over time is achieved by arranging the actions in a way that maximizes happiness over time, and vice versa.

The Relation Between The Ultimate People and The Ultimate World

The Ultimate World (UW) is defined in Characterization 3.2 of UW Theory as "a world-wide team of UPs that work together as a team to maximize group problem solving skill over time." The relation between the UPs and the UW is *a system within a system*. The UPs and the UW utilize feedback by means of control theory, so the underlying theory for each system is control theory. Consequently, the relation between UPs and the UW is *a control system within a control system*, with the UPs being control systems within the UW control system. Control theory needs to be the underlying theory because control theory provides the means to exchange feedback between the UPs and UW for correcting mistakes, adapting to change, dealing with unknowns, maintaining stability, and improving performance over time.

THE PEOPLE

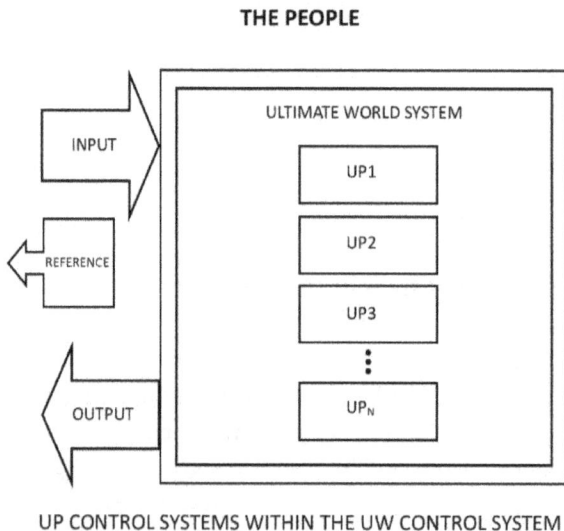

UP CONTROL SYSTEMS WITHIN THE UW CONTROL SYSTEM

This diagram illustrates how the UP control systems fit within the UW control system. UPs are the "system" element of the UW control system. The UW control system elements are detailed in Level 4 of the

UW scientific solution. The UP control system elements are detailed in Level 7 of the UW scientific solution.

As control systems, both the UPs and the UW have the same basic elements: a reference, a controller, an input, an output, and a system. The next two sections provide an overview of the UW elements and the UP elements, respectively.

The Ultimate World Elements

There are five basic elements of the Ultimate World (UW): the UW reference; the UW controller; the UW input, the UW output and the UW system.

The UW Reference

The UW reference is the desired output of the UW, namely UP_{MAX}.

The UW Controller

The UW controller is the Human Survival Problem Solver (HSPS), which is also the controller for the UPs. The HSPS serves as the controller for everything in UW theory. The function of the HSPS is to evaluate the UW and UP outputs and send new UW and UP inputs, with the overall goal of increasing UP_N.

The UW Input

Remember from Chapter 2 that the UW Scientific Problem is:

$$\text{Maximum UW Efficiency} = \frac{UP_{MAX}}{PSA_{MIN}}$$

where the output of the UW scientific problem is UP_{MAX} and the input is PSA_{MIN}.

The primary UW input, therefore, is Problem Solving Actions (PSAs). PSAs are presented to the UW as a list of PSAs, which serve as a solution to the problems identified within each PSA. The goal is to minimize the number of PSAs. Ideally, these PSAs will be performed correctly the first time, and the use of the UW scientific method helps ensure that the PSAs identified are the correct PSAs (i.e. the ones that will lead to successful solution). If the correct PSAs are not performed correctly the first time, a built-in self-correction mechanism will be used to correct any mistakes. This built-in self-correction mechanism is the control theory framework for the UW.

Other UW system inputs in addition to PSAs are: new non-UP certified people; and paychecks. New non-UP certified people are simply people who have not yet been trained and certified as UPs. Paychecks are monetary rewards in return for the successfully completed PSAs. They are the same as the paycheck that one receives from an employer for successfully completing job duties.

The UW Output

The primary UW Output is Ultimate People (UPs). The goal is to maximize the number of UPs. The actual number of UPs, or UP_N, is the actual measure that is sent to the HSPS for comparison to the reference which is UP_{MAX}. At this point, we do not know the exact number of UP_{MAX}. We do know that the universe is incredibly large, much larger than the earth. So we can be reasonably certain that UP_{MAX} is much larger than the current population of the earth. A shorter term goal is to train as many people in the current world to become certified UPs, thereby increasing UP_N over time.

The other system output is performance results on the PSAs by the UPs.

The UW System

The UW System is defined as "uniquely identified UPs from UP1 to UP_N." It is now time to define the UP control system elements in detail.

The Ultimate Person Elements

A UP is defined in Characterization 1.0 of UW Theory (which is the Supreme Characterization of the Supreme Hypothesis). The definition of the UP is "a person who maximizes problem solving skill over time." There are five control theory based elements involved in maximizing problem solving skill over time: the UP reference; the UP controller; the UP input; the UP output; and the UP system.

The UP Reference

The UP reference is the desired output of the UPs. The desired output of the UPs is maximum problem solving skill over time. There are two components of maximum problem solving skill over time: personal problem solving skill and professional problem solving skill. Personal problem solving skill is demonstrated by performance results on personal projects and daily tasks. Professional problem solving skill is demonstrated by performance results on professional (i.e. job-related) projects and daily tasks.

The UP Controller

The UP controller is the same controller as the UW controller. The Human Survival Problem Solver (HSPS), serves as the controller for everything in UW theory. The function of the HSPS is to evaluate UP outputs and send new UP inputs.

The UP Input

The UP system inputs are similar to the UW system inputs, namely, new PSAs and paychecks, with the exception of new non-certified UPs. New non-certified UPs are an input that applies only to the UW.

The UP Output

The single UP system output is performance results on the PSAs.

The UP System

The UP system takes UP inputs and produces UP outputs. The underlying process of converting these inputs to outputs is the Ultimate Person Performance Process (UPPP). Overall, UPPP is a cyclical process for on-going action performance. It is basically a list management process that has six basic steps:

1) Define problem
2) Define solution (actions)
3) Perform solution (actions)
4) Evaluate results
5) Repeat steps 2-4 continuously on new solutions
6) Perfect the UPPP and have fun

Ideally, this UPPP process will be performed with the assistance of the HSPS, the intelligent, computer-based system for solving the human survival problem. However, until the HSPS is developed and implemented, it is necessary to perform the UPPP manually. A manual approach is just using a paper document to establish and maintain a UP Action List. The details of establishing and maintaining a UP Action List are given in a companion book entitled *The Ultimate Person*. There is plenty of computer support available now for assistance in managing the

UP Action List. This computer support is discussed in *The Ultimate Person* book.

Now, it is time to learn the performance rules for maximizing both performance and happiness. But first, we must learn Flow Theory. It's the secret to maximizing both performance results and happiness.

The Happiness/Performance Link

According to Flow Theory, which is an established theory of the psychology of optimal experience (i.e. maximum happiness), action performance and happiness are directly linked. By arranging actions according the guidelines of Flow theory, both individuals and groups can maximize both performance and happiness. In UW, the guidelines (or rules) for both individual and group problem solving are based primarily on Flow theory. They are designed for optimal problem solving performance, and will lead to maximum happiness for both individuals and groups.

Appendix A3 elaborates on Flow theory and provides examples of how Flow is achieved in the real world. A Flow state is characterized by three primary conditions:

> 1) *clear goals* – this provides the necessary structure and direction to the activity
> 2) *clear and immediate feedback* – this helps the person negotiate any challenging demands and allows them to make adjustments to their performance to maintain a Flow state
> 3) *a challenge/skill balance (CS balance)* – this provides a feeling of confidence and control over one's ability to succeed.

This challenge/skill balance diagram on the next page illustrates how the different levels of challenge and skill affect one's mental state.

THE CHALLENGE/SKILL (CS) BALANCE

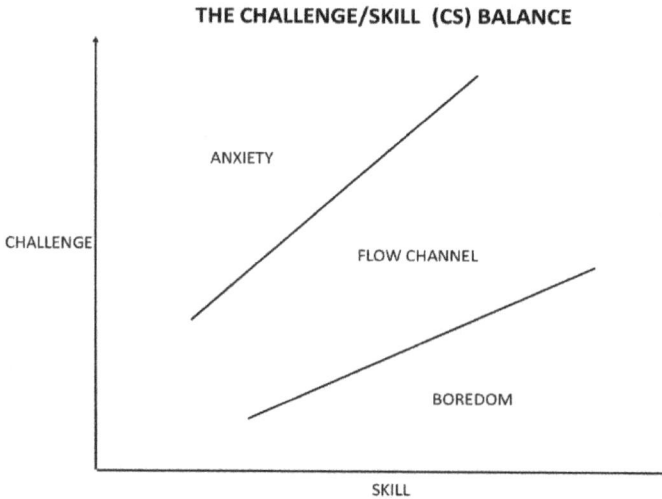

Above is a basic chart that summarizes the challenge/skill (CS) balance. It is a chart of the level of the challenge of a certain action versus the skill level available to meet the challenge. Notice that an activity that has high challenge and low skill leads to a state of anxiety or being stressed out because that action cannot be performed. Anxiety has a negative effect on performance because it can cause frustration with an activity that will eventually cause a person to give up and quit the activity.

An activity that has low challenge and high skill leads to a state of boredom because the activity is too easily performed. Boredom has a negative effect on performance because it can cause a person to lose interest and eventually quit the activity. In both states – anxiety and boredom – the key performance problem is lost attention and focus on the activity.

By contrast, the CS balance or "flow channel" has a positive effect on performance because a person is succeeding at an activity and increasing skill over time, so that higher levels of performance can be achieved over time. In a Flow state, attention and focus on the activity are maximized.

There are many other psychological benefits to optimal action performance including self-esteem, self-confidence, and an increased learning capacity. There is also evidence that these psychological benefits have medical benefits as well, although medical issues are beyond the scope of this book.

Performance Rules

UPPP uses performance rules designed to maximize performance in a way that also leads to maximum happiness. There are four primary performance rules for all UPs. These performance rules are based on the three conditions of Flow mentioned above, plus safety awareness. Here is the list of performance rules:

> Performance Rule #1 Clearly identify PSAs
> Performance Rule #2 Obtain feedback on progress
> Performance Rule #3 Maintain a challenge/skill balance
> Performance Rule #4 Maintain safety awareness

Performance Rule #1 Clearly identify PSAs.

Performance Rule #1 is necessary because clear goals are a condition of Flow. The UW scientific method is used to identify all PSAs. It starts by identifying all of the eleven PSA data fields for each PSA.

Performance Rule #2 Obtain feedback on progress

Performance Rule #2 is necessary because feedback on progress is a condition of Flow. Feedback is defined as information about a person's performance of a task, which is used as a basis for improvement. In UW Theory, feedback is the performance results on the PSAs by the UPs.

Performance Rule #3 Maintain challenge/skill balance

Performance Rule #3 is necessary because a CS balance is a condition of Flow. It involves making adjustments to both the challenge and skill level to stay in a flow state, thereby avoiding the states of anxiety and boredom. There are three basic guidelines for maintaining a CS balance:

> 1) *if you are in a state of anxiety, then either decrease challenge or increase skill or both.* Ways to decrease challenge is to perform less PSAs in more time. Ways to increase skill are: a) try again (practice makes perfect); b) break down PSAs into PSAs that are more doable. This can be accomplished by getting how-to information on the problem from an expert (either online or local); or c) get UP skill training or re-training.
> 2) *if you are in a state of boredom, then increase challenge.* Ways to increase challenge include performing more PSAs in less time.
> 3) *always increase skill.* Increasing skill is always necessary to maintain a CS balance over time. This is because increasing skill is a strategy that will always move one closer to the CS balance *over time*, regardless of whether one is stressed out or bored. Life's challenges have a way of increasing themselves on their own.

Performance Rule #4 Maintain Safety Awareness

Performance Rule #4 is necessary because a Flow state can result in complete absorption of a person's attention. One must always maintain awareness of their surroundings to be able to respond to safety hazards. Texting while driving is a common example of a safety hazard that results from not maintaining awareness of one's surroundings.

Special Rules for Group Performance

The four individual performance rules mentioned above also apply to groups, so the first group performance rule is "apply the four individual performance rules to the group." There are also three additional performance rules that apply to group problem solving, although these group performance rules should also be considered by individuals. Here are the four group performance rules:

> Group Performance Rule #1 Apply the Four Individual Performance Rules to the Group
> Group Performance Rule #2 Utilize a Best Practices Democracy.
> Group Performance Rule #3 Localize Your Activity
> Group Performance Rule #4 Communicate with Credibility.

Group Performance Rule #1 Apply the Four Individual Performance Rules to the Group.

Group Performance Rule #1 is necessary because the individual performance rules also apply to groups. This means that groups should also: clearly identify PSAs, obtain feedback on progress; maintain a CS balance; and maintain safety awareness. Note that the primary group (or world) PSA is UP_{MAX}, the primary group (or world) feedback is UP_N, and the primary way to maintain group (or world) CS balance is by increasing group problem solving skill over time.

Group Performance Rule #2 Utilize a Best Practices Democracy.

Group Performance Rule #2 is necessary because the basic tenants of a democracy - free speech, equal opportunity, fair competition, and rule of law - are necessary to maximize group performance. Since the HSPS is the future technology for group problem solving, these basic tenants of a best practices democracy need to be programmed into the HSPS.

Group Performance Rule #3 Localize the Activity

Group Performance Rule #3 is necessary because all UPs must obey local laws. All UPs should also consult with local professionals, including legal and financial professionals before putting anything in UW Theory into practice.

Group Performance Rule #4 Communicate with Credibility

Group Performance Rule #4 is necessary because credible communication is necessary to correctly identify and perform all PSAs within UW Theory. This means that the UW Experiment Form should be used for all formal communication. See Chapter 6 for more detail on the UW Experiment Form, and on the future of communication.

IMPORTANT NOTE: The UW People Scientific Solution now continues at Level 4.

The UW People Scientific Solution

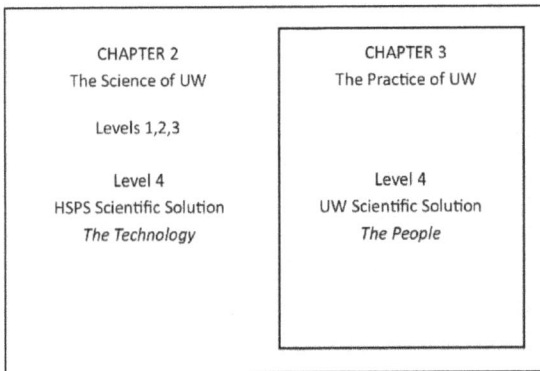

Remember that Level 4 of the UW Scientific Solution branches off into two parts, the technology issues (i.e. the HSPS), and the people issues (i.e. the UW). The scientific solution of the UW Technology (i.e. the HSPS) is given in chapter 2, and the scientific solution of the UW People is given here.

THE UW SCIENTIFIC SOLUTION

CHAPTER 2 The Science of UW Levels 1,2,3 Level 4 HSPS Scientific Solution *The Technology*	CHAPTER 3 The Practice of UW Level 4 UW Scientific Solution *The People*

CHAPTER CONTENT DIAGRAM

This diagram illustrates how the UW Scientific Solution branches into two parts at Level 4. One part is the HSPS Scientific Solution in Chapter 2. The other part is the UW Scientific Solution in Chapter 3. Both parts are based on the same UW science, which is defined in Chapter 2. Levels 1, 2, and 3 of the UW Scientific Solution are also given in Chapter 2.

The UW Level 4 Scientific Solution

The UW Level 4 solution is defined by first sub-dividing the Level 3 problems into the Level 4 sub-problems. Then the

UW scientific method is used to formulate the Level 4 character-izations and Level 4 hypotheses. The Level 4 hypotheses serve as the Level 4 scientific solution. Here are the steps involved:

> Step 1 – Problem 3.2 The Ultimate World is sub-divided into the following sub-problems: Problem UR4.1 UW reference; Problem UC4.1 UW controller; Problem UI4.1 UW input; Problem UO4.1 UW output; and Problem US4.1 UW system.

> Step 2 – The Level 4 characterizations and hypotheses are defined as follows:

The UW Level 4 Characterizations

Characterization ID# = [CUR4.1]
PSA ID# = [PSA UR4.1]
PSA name = [Establish and maintain a reference within UW]
Problem ID# = [Problem UR4.1]
Problem name [Reference within UW]
Action name = [Establish and maintain]
Reason for necessity = [Because a reference is a necessary ele-ment of control theory]
Unit of analysis = [Ultimate World (UW)]
Time deadline = [No time deadline (i.e. infinity)]
Success measure = [UP$_{MAX}$]
Supplemental definitions = 1. [Reference – the primary purpose the reference is to serve as the desired output of the system] 2. [The UW reference is UP$_{MAX}$]

Characterization ID# = [CUC4.1]
PSA ID# = [PSA UC4.1]
PSA name = [Establish and maintain a controller for the UW]
Problem ID# = [Problem UC4.1]
Problem name [Controller within UW]
Action name = [Establish and maintain]

Reason for necessity = [Because a controller is a necessary element of control theory]
Unit of analysis = [Ultimate World (UW)]
Time deadline = [No time deadline (i.e. infinity)]
Success measure = [Error free management of all UW solutions]
Supplemental definitions = 1. [Controller – the primary purpose of a controller is to take the output of a system (i.e. the actual output), compare the output to the reference (i.e. the desired output), make corrections to this output if necessary, and then send new input to a system] 2. [The UW controller is the HSPS]

Characterization ID# = [CUI4.1]
PSA ID# = [PSA UI4.1]
PSA name = [Establish and maintain an input to the UW]
Problem ID# = [Problem UI4.1]
Problem name [Input within UW]
Action name = [Establish and maintain]
Reason for necessity = [Because an input is a necessary element of control theory]
Unit of analysis = [Ultimate World (UW)]
Time deadline = [No time deadline (i.e. infinity)]
Success measure = [Error free supply of the UW inputs]
Supplemental definitions = 1. [Input- The purpose of the input is to supply the system with information that is then processed by the system.] 2. [The UW there are three primary inputs to the UW system: 1) new PSAs; 2) paychecks; and 3) Non-UP certified people]

Characterization ID# = [CUO4.1]
PSA ID# = [PSA UO4.1]
PSA name = [Establish and maintain an output from the UW]
Problem ID# = [Problem UO4.1]
Problem name [Output within UW]
Action name = [Establish and maintain]
Reason for necessity = [Because an output is a necessary element of control theory]
Unit of analysis = [Ultimate World (UW)]

Time deadline = [No time deadline (i.e. infinity)]
Success measure = [Error free transfer of the UW output to the UW controller]
Supplemental definitions = 1. [Output- The purpose of the system output is to transfer the outputs of the UW to the UW controller.] 2. [The UW there are two primary UW system outputs: 1) performance results; and 2) UP_N]

Characterization ID# = [CUS4.1]
PSA ID# = [PSA US4.1]
PSA name = [Establish and maintain a system within UW]
Problem ID# = [Problem US4.1]
Problem name [System within UW]
Action name = [Establish and maintain]
Reason for Necessity = [Because a system is a necessary element of control theory]
Unit of analysis = [Ultimate World (UW)]
Time deadline = [No time deadline (i.e. infinity)]
Success measure = [Error free processing of the UW inputs]
Supplemental definitions = 1. [System - The purpose of the UW system is to process the system input, and convert it to system output] 2. [The UW system is composed of uniquely identified UPs numbered UP1 through UP_N. UP_N is the actual number of UPs.]

The UW Level 4 Hypotheses

> Hypothesis ID# = [HUR4.1]
> HUR4.1 Establishing and maintaining a reference for the UW is a necessary action because a reference is a necessary element of control theory.

> Hypothesis ID# = [HUC4.1]
> HUC4.1 Establishing and maintaining a controller for the UW is a necessary action because a controller is a necessary element of control theory.

Hypothesis ID# = [HUI4.1]
HUI4.1 Establishing and maintaining an input to the UW is a necessary action because an input is a necessary element of control theory.

Hypothesis ID# = [HUO4.1]
HUO4.1 Establishing and maintaining an output from the UW is a necessary action because an output is a necessary element of control theory.

Hypothesis ID# = [HUS4.1]
HUS4.1 Establishing and maintaining a system within the UW is a necessary action because a system is a necessary element of control theory.

THE PEOPLE

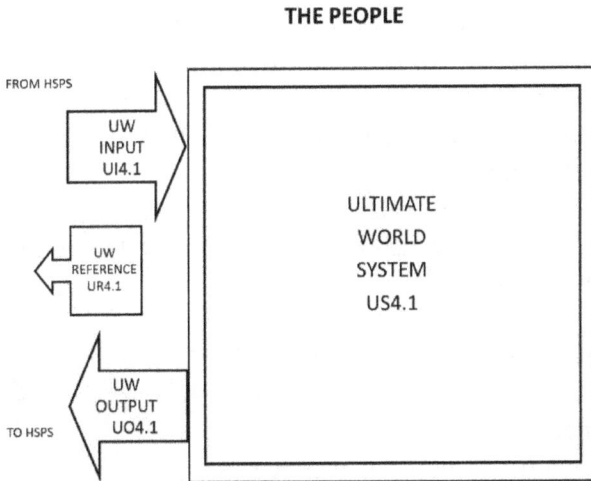

UW LEVEL 4 DIAGRAM

The UW Level 4 diagram illustrates the five elements of the UW control system: the UW reference; the UW controller; the UW input; the UW output, and the UW system. Note that all UW elements have a "U" prefix in their problem ID#. The UW controller ID# = UC4.1. The UW reference ID# = UR4.1. The UW input ID# = UI4.1. The UW output ID# = UO4.1. And the UW system ID# = US4.1. Also note that only the links to the UW controller are shown here. The UW controller is the HSPS which is detailed in Chapter 2.

The UW Level 5 Scientific Solution

The UW Level 5 solution is defined by first sub-dividing the Level 4 problems into the Level 5 sub-problems. Then the UW scientific method is used to formulate the Level 5 character-izations and Level 5 hypotheses. The Level 5 hypotheses serve as the Level 5 scientific solution. Here are the steps involved:

Step 1 – Problem UR4.1 UW reference is subdivided into sub-problem UR5.1 UW reference elements. Problem UC4.1 UW controller is sub-divided into sub-problem UC5.1 controller elements. Problem UI4.1 UW input is sub-divided into sub-problem UI5.1 UW input elements. Problem UO4.1 UW output is sub-divided into sub-prob-lem UO5.1 UW output elements. Problem US4.1 UW system is sub-divided into sub-problem US5.1 UW sys-tem elements.

Step 2 – The Level 5 characterizations and hypotheses are defined as follows:

The UW Level 5 Characterizations

UW Reference Elements

Characterization ID# = [CUR5.1]
PSA ID# = [PSA UR5.1]
PSA name = [Establish and maintain UP_{MAX} as the UW refer-ence]
Problem ID# = [Problem UR5.1]
Problem name [UP_{MAX} as UW reference]
Action name = [Establish and maintain]

Reason for necessity = [Because UP$_{MAX}$ is the desired output of the UW system]
Unit of analysis = [Ultimate World (UW)]
Time deadline = [No time deadline (i.e. infinity)]
Success measure = [Maximum number of UPs]
Supplemental definitions = 1. [Reference – the desired output of the system.] 2. [The UW desired output is UP$_{MAX}$]

UW Controller Elements

Characterization ID# = [CUC5.1]
PSA ID# = [PSA UC5.1]
PSA name = [HSPS as the UW controller]
Problem ID# = [Problem UC5.1]
Problem name [New PSAs]
Action name = [Establish and maintain]
Reason for necessity = [Because the HSPS is the primary controller within UW Theory]
Unit of analysis = [Ultimate World (UW)]
Time deadline = [No time deadline (i.e. infinity)]
Success measure = [Correct solutions sent from the HSPS to the UW]
Supplemental definitions = 1.[Controller – the primary purpose of a controller is to take the output of a system (i.e. the actual output), compare the output to the reference (i.e. the desired output), make corrections to this output if necessary, and then send new input to a system.] 2. [The UW controller is the HSPS]

UW Input Elements

Characterization ID# = [CUI5.1]
PSA ID# = [PSA UI5.1]
PSA name = [Establish and maintain new PSAs]
Problem ID# = [Problem UI5.1]
Problem name [New PSAs]
Action name = [Establish and maintain]

Reason for necessity = [Because new PSAs are necessary for solving new problems, and new problems are an on-going issue in the UW]
Unit of analysis = [Ultimate World (UW)]
Time deadline = [No time deadline (i.e. infinity)]
Success measure = [Correct PSAs sent from the HSPS to the UW]
Supplemental definitions = [Correct PSAs – PSAs that are doable for UPs on their first try]

Characterization ID# = [CUI5.2]
PSA ID# = [PSA UI5.2]
PSA name = [Establish and maintain paychecks]
Problem ID# = [Problem UI5.2]
Problem name [Paychecks]
Action name = [Establish and maintain]
Reason for necessity = [Because paychecks are a necessary exchange from the HSPS to the UPs for the UPs successful completion of PSAs]
Unit of analysis = [Ultimate World (UW)]
Time deadline = [No time deadline (i.e. infinity)]
Success measure = [Paychecks are measured in terms of money and the amount of money depends on the specific nature of the problem solved by the UP]
Supplemental definitions = [Paychecks – money in exchange for successful completion of PSAs by the UPs]

Characterization ID# = [CUI5.3]
PSA ID# = [PSA UI5.3]
PSA name = [Establish and maintain new non-UP certified people]
Problem ID# = [Problem UI5.3]
Problem name [New Non-UP certified people]
Action name = [Establish and maintain]
Reason for necessity = [Because new non-UP certified people are necessary achieve UP_{MAX}]
Unit of analysis = [Ultimate World (UW)]

Time deadline = [No time deadline (i.e. infinity)]
Success measure = [Indefinite supply of new non-UP certified people]
Supplemental definitions = [New non-UP certified people – new people who have not been trained, and certified as UPs]

UW Output Elements

Characterization ID# = [CUO5.1]
PSA ID# = [PSA UO5.1]
PSA name = [Establish and maintain performance results]
Problem ID# = [Problem UO5.1]
Problem name [Performance results]
Action name = [Establish and maintain]
Reason for necessity = [Because performance results are necessary feedback from the individual UPs on their performance on actual PSAs.]
Unit of analysis = [Ultimate World (UW)]
Time deadline = [No time deadline (i.e. infinity)]
Success measure = [Successful performance results]
Supplemental definitions = [Performance Results – the actual output of the individual UPs performance on the PSAs. This output is sent to the HSPS for evaluation and determination of the paychecks and the new PSAs.]

Characterization ID# = [CUO5.2]
PSA ID# = [PSA UO5.2]
PSA name = [Establish and maintain UP_N]
Problem ID# = [Problem UO5.2]
Problem name [UP_N]
Action name = [Establish and maintain]
Reason for necessity = [Because UP_N is necessary feedback to determine the progress of the UW]
Unit of analysis = [Ultimate World (UW)]
Time deadline = [No time deadline (i.e. infinity)]
Success Measure = [Maximum increase of UP_N]

UW System Elements

Characterization ID# = [CUS5.1]
PSA ID# = [PSA US5.1]
PSA name = [Establish and maintain uniquely identified UPs from UP1 to UP_N]
Problem ID# = [Problem US5.1]
Problem name [Uniquely identified UPs from UP1 to UP_N]
Action name = [Establish and maintain]
Reason for necessity = [Because uniquely identified UPs are necessary to ensure that each UP is performing PSAs in an optimal fashion, and is experiencing maximum paychecks and happiness]
Unit of analysis = [Ultimate World (UW)]
Time deadline = [No time deadline (i.e. infinity)]
Success Measure = [Unique identity for each UP]

The UW Level 5 Hypotheses

UW Reference Hypothesis

Hypothesis ID# = [HUR5.1]
HUR5.1 Establishing and maintaining UP_{MAX} as the UW reference is a necessary action because UP_{MAX} is the desired output of the UW system.

UW Controller Hypothesis

Hypothesis ID# = [HUC5.1]
HUC5.1 Establishing and maintaining HSPS as the controller of the UW is a necessary action because the HSPS is the primary controller within UW Theory.

UW Input Hypotheses

Hypothesis ID# = [HUI5.1]

HUI5.1 Establishing and maintaining new PSAs is a necessary action because new PSAs are necessary for solving new problems, and new problems are an on-going issue in the UW.

Hypothesis ID# = [HUI5.2]
HUI5.2 Establishing and maintaining paychecks is a necessary action because paychecks are a necessary exchange from the HSPS to the UPs for the UPs successful completion of PSAs.

Hypothesis ID# = [HUI5.3]
HUI5.3 Establishing and maintaining new non-UPs is a necessary action because new non-UP certified people are necessary achieve UP_{MAX}.

UW Output Hypotheses

Hypothesis ID# = [HUO5.1]
HUO5.1 Establishing and maintaining performance results is a necessary action because performance results are necessary feedback from the individual UPs on their performance on actual PSAs.

Hypothesis ID# = [HUO5.2]
HUO5.2 Establishing and maintaining UP_N is a necessary action because UP_N is necessary feedback to determine the progress of the UW.

UW System Hypothesis

Hypothesis ID# = [HUS5.1]
HUS5.1 Establishing and maintaining uniquely identified UPs from UP1 to UP_N is a necessary action because uniquely identified UPs are necessary to ensure that each UP is performing PSAs in an optimal fashion, and is experiencing maximum paychecks and happiness.

THE PEOPLE

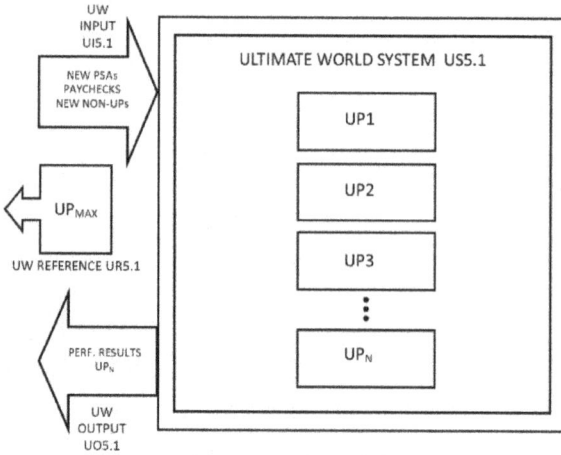

UW LEVEL 5 DIAGRAM

The UW Level 5 diagram identifies the five elements of the UW control system: the UW reference (UP$_{MAX}$) ID# UR5.1; the UW controller (HSPS) ID# UC5.1 (not pictured here); the UW inputs (new PSAs, paychecks, non-certified UPs) ID# UI5.1-UI5.3; the UW outputs (performance results, UP$_N$) ID# UO5.1-UO5.2; and the UW system (UP1-UP$_N$) ID# US5.1.

The UW Level 6 Scientific Solution

The UW Level 6 solution is defined by first sub-dividing the Level 5 problems into the Level 6 sub-problems. Then the UW scientific method is used to formulate the Level 6 characterizations and Level 6 hypotheses. The Level 6 hypotheses serve as the Level 6 scientific solution. Here are the steps involved:

Step 1 – Problem HUS5.1 UW system elements is subdivided into sub-problem UP control system elements: UP reference UPR6.1; UP controller UPC6.1; UP input UPI6.1; UP output UPO6.1; and UP system UPS6.1

Step 2 – The Level 6 characterizations and hypotheses are defined as follows:

The UW Level 6 Characterizations

UP Reference

Characterization ID# = [CUPR6.1]
PSA ID# = [PSA UPR6.1]
PSA name = [Establish and maintain a reference for each UP]
Problem ID# = [Problem UPR6.1]
Problem name [Reference for each UP]
Action name = [Establish and maintain]
Reason for necessity = [Because a reference is a necessary element of control theory]
Unit of analysis = [Ultimate Person (UP)]
Time deadline = [No time deadline (i.e. infinity)]
Success measure = [Maximum problem solving skill over time]
Supplemental definitions = [Reference – the primary purpose the reference is to serve as the desired output of the system. The UP reference is maximum problem solving skill over time. The three types of problem solving skill are: 1) personal problem solving skill; and 2) professional problem solving skill]

UP Controller

Characterization ID# = [CUPC6.1]
PSA ID# = [PSA UPC6.1]
PSA name = [Establish and maintain a controller for each of the UPs]
Problem ID# = [Problem UPC6.1]
Problem name [Controller for each UP]
Action name = [Establish and maintain]
Reason for necessity = [Because a controller is a necessary element of control theory]
Unit of analysis = [Ultimate Person (UP)]
Time deadline = [No time deadline (i.e. infinity)]

Success measure = [Error free management of all UP inputs]
Supplemental definitions = 1. [Controller – the primary purpose
of a controller is to take the output of a system (i.e. the actual
output), compare the output to the reference (i.e. the desired output), make corrections to this output if necessary, and then send
new input to a system.] 2. [The UP controller is the Human Survival Problem Solver (HSPS)]

UP Input

Characterization ID# = [CUPI6.1]
PSA ID# = [PSA UPI6.1]
PSA name = [Establish and maintain an input for each UP]
Problem ID# = [Problem UPI6.1]
Problem name [Input for each UP]
Action name = [Establish and maintain]
Reason for necessity = [Because an input is a necessary element
of control theory]
Unit of analysis = [Ultimate Person (UP)]
Time deadline = [No time deadline (i.e. infinity)]
Success measure = [Error free supply of the UW inputs]
Supplemental definitions = 1. [Input- the purpose of the system
input is to supply the system with information that is then pro-
cessed by the system.] 2. [The UW there are two primary inputs
to each UP system: 1) new PSAs; and 2) paychecks]

UP Output

Characterization ID# = [CUPO6.1]
PSA ID# = [PSA UPO6.1]
PSA name = [Establish and maintain an output for each UP]
Problem ID# = [Problem UPO6.1]
Problem name [Output for each UP]
Action name = [Establish and maintain]
Reason for necessity = [Because an output is a necessary element
of control theory]
Unit of analysis = [Ultimate Person (UP)]

Time deadline = [No time deadline (i.e. infinity)]
Success measure = [Error free transfer of the UP output to the UP controller]
Supplemental definitions = 1. [Output- The purpose of the output is to transfer the outputs of the UPs to the UP controller.] 2. [The UW there are two primary UP outputs: personal performance results and professional performance results.]

UP System

Characterization ID# = [CUPS6.1]
PSA ID# = [PSA UPS6.1]
PSA name = [Establish and maintain a system for each UP]
Problem ID# = [Problem UPS6.1]
Problem name [System within UW]
Action name = [Establish and maintain]
Reason for necessity = [Because a system is a necessary element of control theory]
Unit of analysis = [Ultimate Person (UP)]
Time deadline = [No time deadline (i.e. infinity)]
Success measure = [Error free processing of the UP inputs]
Supplemental definitions = [System - The purpose of the UP system is to process the input, and convert it to the output. The UP system is composed of the Ultimate Person Performance Process.]

The UW Level 6 Hypotheses

UP Control System Elements

Hypothesis ID# = [HUPR6.1]
HUPR6.1 Establishing and maintaining a reference for each UP is a necessary action because a reference is a necessary element of control theory.

Hypothesis ID# = [HUPC6.1]

HUPC6.1 Establishing and maintaining a controller for each UP is a necessary action because a controller is a necessary element of control

Hypothesis ID# = [HUPI6.1]
HUPI6.1 Establishing and maintaining an input for each UP is a necessary action because a system input is a necessary element of control theory.

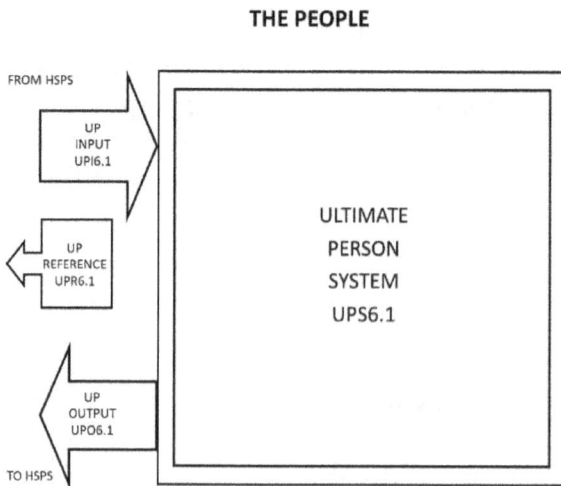

Hypothesis ID# = [HUPO6.1]
HUPO6.1 Establishing and maintaining an output for each UP is a necessary action because a system output is a necessary element of control theory.

Hypothesis ID# = [HUPS6.1]
HUPS6.1 Establishing and maintaining a system for each UP is a necessary action because a system is a necessary element of control theory.

THE PEOPLE

FROM HSPS

UP
INPUT
UPI6.1

ULTIMATE

UP
REFERENCE
UPR6.1

PERSON

SYSTEM

UPS6.1

UP
OUTPUT
UPO6.1

TO HSPS

UW LEVEL 6 DIAGRAM

The UW Level 6 diagram illustrates the five elements of the UP control system: the UP reference ID# = UPR6.1; the UP controller ID# =

UPC6.1; the UP input ID# = UPI6.1; the UP output ID# = UPO6.1; and the UP system ID# = UPS6.1. Note that only the links to the UP controller is shown here. The UP controller is HSPS, which is detailed in chapter 2.

The UW Level 7 Scientific Solution

The UW Level 7 solution is defined by first sub-dividing the Level 6 problems into the Level 6 sub-problems. Then the UW scientific method is used to formulate the Level 7 characterizations and Level 7 hypotheses. The Level 7 hypotheses serve as the Level 7 scientific solution. Here are the steps involved:

Step 1 – Problem UPR6.1 UW reference is subdivided into sub-problem UPR7.1 UW reference elements. Problem UPC6.1 UW controller is sub-divided into sub-problem UPC7.1 controller elements. Problem UPI6.1 UW input is sub-divided into sub-problem UPI7.1 UW input elements. Problem UPO6.1 UW output is sub-divided into sub-problem UPO7.1 UW output elements. Problem UPS6.1 UW system is sub-divided into sub-problem UPS7.1 UW system elements.

Step 2 – The Level 7 characterizations and hypotheses are defined as follows:

The UW Level 7 Characterizations

UP Reference Elements

Characterization ID# = [CUPR7.1]
PSA ID# = [PSA UPR7.1]
PSA name = [Establish and maintain maximum personal problem solving skill, and maximum professional problem solving skill as the UP reference]
Problem ID# = [Problem UPR7.1]

Problem name [Maximum personal problem solving skill and maximum professional problem solving skill as the UP reference]

Action name = [Establish and maintain]

Reason for necessity = [Because maximum personal problem solving skill and maximum professional problem solving skill are the desired outputs of the UP system]

Unit of analysis = [Ultimate Person (UP)]

Time deadline = [No time deadline (i.e. infinity)]

Success measure = [Maximum personal problem solving skill and maximum professional problem solving skill]

Supplemental definitions = [1) personal problem solving skill is based on mastery of personal projects and daily tasks, 2) professional problem solving skill is based on mastery of professional projects and daily tasks]

UP Controller Elements

Characterization ID# = [CUPC7.1]

PSA ID# = [PSA UPC7.1]

PSA name = [Establish and maintain HSPS as the UP controller]

Problem ID# = [Problem UPC7.1]

Problem name [New PSAs]

Action name = [Establish and maintain]

Reason for necessity = [Because the HSPS is the primary controller within all of UW Theory]

Unit of analysis = [Ultimate Person (UP)]

Time deadline = [No time deadline (i.e. infinity)]

Success measure = [Correct PSAs sent from the HSPS to each UP]

Supplemental definitions = 1. [Controller – the primary purpose of a controller is to take the output of a system (i.e. the actual output), compare the output to the reference (i.e. the desired output), make corrections to this output if necessary, and then send new input to a system] 2. [Each of the UP controllers is the HSPS]

UP Input Elements

Characterization ID# = [CUPI7.1]
PSA ID# = [PSA UPI7.1]
PSA name = [Establish and maintain new PSAs and paychecks as the UP inputs]
Problem ID# = [Problem UPI7.1]
Problem name [New PSAs]
Action name = [Establish and maintain]
Reason for necessity = [Because new PSAs and paychecks are necessary inputs for solving new problems, and new problems are an on-going issue for each UP]
Unit of analysis = [Ultimate Person (UP)]
Time deadline = [No time deadline (i.e. infinity)]
Success measure = [Correct PSAs sent from the HSPS to each UP]
Supplemental definitions = [Correct PSAs – PSAs that are doable by UPs on their first try]

UP Output Elements

Characterization ID# = [CUPO7.1]
PSA ID# = [PSA UPO7.1]
PSA name = [Establish and maintain personal and professional problem solving skill performance results as a UP output]
Problem ID# = [Problem UPO7.1]
Problem name [Personal and professional problem solving skill performance results]
Action name = [Establish and maintain]
Reason for necessity = [Because personal and professional problem solving skill performance results are necessary feedback from each of the individual UPs on their performance on actual PSAs.]
Unit of analysis = [Ultimate Person (UP)]
Time deadline = [No time deadline (i.e. infinity)]
Success measure = [Successful performance results]

Supplemental definitions = [Performance Results – the actual output of the individual UPs performance on the PSAs. This output is sent to the HSPS for evaluation and determination of the paychecks and the new PSAs.]

UP System Elements

Characterization ID# = [CUPS7.1]
PSA ID# = [PSA UPS7.1]
PSA name = [Establish and maintain the Ultimate Person Performance Process (UPPP) as the UP system]
Problem ID# = [Problem UPS7.1]
Problem name [Ultimate Person Performance Process]
Action name = [Establish and maintain]
Reason for necessity = [Because the Ultimate Person Performance Process is necessary to maximize the performance and happiness of each UP]
Unit of analysis = [Ultimate Person (UP)]
Time deadline = [No time deadline (i.e. infinity)]
Success measure = [Maximum Performance and Maximum Happiness from each UP]
Supplemental definitions = [UPPP is an action list management process that has six steps: 1) define problem, 2) define solution (PSAs), 3) perform solution (PSAs), 4) evaluate results, 5) repeat steps 2-4 continuously on new solutions, and 6) perfect the UPPP and have fun]

The UW Level 7 Hypotheses

UP Reference Hypothesis

Hypothesis ID# = [HUPR7.1]
HUPR7.1 Establishing and maintaining maximum personal and professional problem solving skill as the UP reference is a necessary action because maximum personal and professional problem solving skill are the desired outputs of the UP system.

UP Controller Hypothesis

Hypothesis ID# = [HUPC7.1]
HUPC7.1 Establishing and maintaining HSPS as the controller
for each UP is a necessary action because the HSPS is the primary controller for all of UW Theory.

UP Input Hypothesis

Hypothesis ID# = [HUPI7.1]
HUPI7.1 Establishing and maintaining new PSAs and paychecks
as inputs to each UP is a necessary action because new PSAs and
paychecks are necessary inputs for solving new problems, and
solving new problems is an on-going issue for each UP.
UP Output Hypothesis

Hypothesis ID# = [HUPO7.1]
HUPO7.1 Establishing and maintaining personal and professional problem solving skill performance results as the UP output
is a necessary action because personal and professional problem
solving skill performance results are necessary feedback from the
individual UPs on their performance on actual PSAs.

UP System Hypothesis

Hypothesis ID# = [HUPS7.1]
HPPS7.1 Establishing and maintaining the Ultimate Person Performance Process (UPPP) as the UP system is a necessary action
because the UPPP is necessary to maximize the performance and
happiness of each UP.

THE PEOPLE

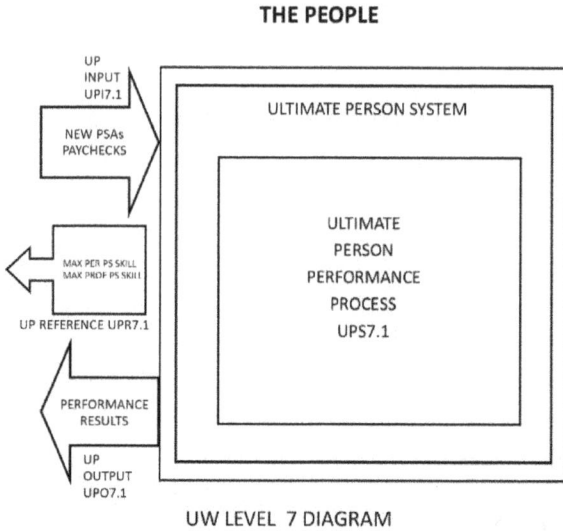

UW LEVEL 7 DIAGRAM

The UW Level 7 diagram illustrates the identities of each of the five elements of the UP control system: the UP reference (maximum personal problem solving skill, maximum professional problem solving skill) ID# = UPR7.1; the UP controller (HSPS) ID# = UPC7.1; the UP inputs (new PSAs, paychecks) ID# = UPI7.1; the UP outputs (personal and professional problem solving skill performance results) ID# = UPO7.1; and the UP system (UPPP) ID# = UPS7.1. And remember, the UP controller is the HSPS, which is detailed in Chapter 2.

The UW Level 8 Scientific Solution

The UW Level 8 solution is defined by first sub-dividing the Level 7 problems into the Level 8 sub-problems. Then the UW scientific method is used to formulate the Level 8 characterizations and Level 8 hypotheses. The Level 8 hypotheses serve as the Level 8 scientific solution. Here are the steps involved:

Step 1 – Problem UPS7.1 UP system elements is sub-divided into sub-problem UPPP elements: Step 1 define problem UPSU8.1; Step 2 define solution (PSAs) UPSU8.2; Step 3 perform solution (PSAs) UPSU8.3; Step 4 evaluate results UPSU8.4; Step 5 repeat steps 2-4 continuously on new solutions UPSU8.5; Step 6 perfect the UPPP and have fun UPSU8.6; and performance rules UUPR8.1

Step 2 – The Level 8 characterizations and hypotheses are defined as follows:

The UW Level 8 Characterizations

UPPP Elements

Characterization ID# = [CUPSU8.1]
PSA ID# = [PSA UPSU8.1]
PSA name = [Establish and maintain "Define problem" as Step 1 of the UPPP]
Problem ID# = [Problem UPSU8.1]
Problem name [Define problem as Step 1 of the UPPP]
Action name = [Establish and maintain]
Reason for necessity = [Because define problem is a necessary first step of maximizing performance and happiness]
Unit of analysis = [Ultimate Person (UP)]
Time deadline = [No time deadline (i.e. infinity)]
Success measure = [Correct definition of problems]

Characterization ID# = [CUPSU8.2]
PSA ID# = [PSA UPSU8.2]
PSA name = [Establish and maintain "Define solution (PSAs)" as Step 2 of the UPPP]
Problem ID# = [Problem UPSU8.2]
Problem name [Define solution (PSAs) as Step 2 of the UPPP]
Action name = [Establish and maintain]

Reason for necessity = [Because Define solution (PSAs) is a nec-
essary second step of maximizing performance and happiness]
Unit of analysis = [Ultimate Person (UP)]
Time deadline = [No time deadline (i.e. infinity)]
Success Measure = [Correct definition of solution (PSAs)]

Characterization ID# = [CUPSU8.3]
PSA ID# = [PSA UPSU8.3]
PSA name = [Establish and maintain "Perform solution (PSAs)"
as Step 3 of the UPPP]
Problem ID# = [Problem UPSU8.3]
Problem name [Perform solution (PSAs) as Step 3 of the UPPP]
Action name = [Establish and maintain]
Reason for necessity = [Because Perform solution (PSAs) is a
necessary third step of maximizing performance and happiness]
Unit of analysis = [Ultimate Person (UP)]
Time deadline = [No time deadline (i.e. infinity)]
Success measure = [Correct performance of solution (PSAs)]

Characterization ID# = [CUPSU8.4]
PSA ID# = [PSA UPSU8.4]
PSA name = [Establish and maintain "Evaluate results" as Step
4 of the UPPP]
Problem ID# = [Problem UPSU8.4]
Problem name [Evaluate results as Step 4 of the UPPP]
Action name = [Establish and maintain]
Reason for necessity = [Because Evaluate results is a necessary
fourth step of maximizing performance and happiness]
Unit of analysis = [Ultimate Person (UP)]
Time deadline = [No time deadline (i.e. infinity)]
Success Measure = [Correct evaluation of results]
Supplemental definitions = [none]

Characterization ID# = [CUPSU8.5]
PSA ID# = [PSA UPSU8.5]
PSA name = [Establish and maintain "Repeat steps 2-4 continu-
ously on new solutions" as Step 5 of the UPPP]

Problem ID# = [Problem UPSU8.5]
Problem name [Repeat steps 2-4 continuously on new solutions as Step 5 of the UPPP]
Action name = [Establish and maintain]
Reason for necessity = [Because Repeat steps 2-4 continuously on new solutions is a necessary fifth step of maximizing performance and happiness]
Unit of analysis = [Ultimate Person (UP)]
Time deadline = [No time deadline (i.e. infinity)]
Success Measure = [Correct ongoing performance of steps 2-4 on new solutions]
Supplemental definitions = [none]

Characterization ID# = [CUPSU8.6]
PSA ID# = [PSA UPSU8.6]
PSA name = [Establish and maintain "Perfect the UPPP and have fun" as Step 6 of the UPPP]
Problem ID# = [Problem UPSU8.6]
Problem name [Perfect the UPPP and have fun as Step 6 of the UPPP]
Action name = [Establish and maintain]
Reason for necessity = [Because Perfect the UPPP and have fun is a necessary fourth step of maximizing performance and happiness]
Unit of analysis = [Ultimate Person (UP)]
Time deadline = [No time deadline (i.e. infinity)]
Success Measure = [Correct performance of the UPPP and maximum happiness]
Supplemental definitions = [none]

Performance Rules Element

Characterization ID# = [CUPSPR8.1]
PSA ID# = [PSA UPSPR8.1]
PSA name = [Establish and maintain performance rules]
Problem ID# = [Problem UPSPR8.1]
Problem name [Performance Rules]

Action name = [Establish and maintain]
Reason for necessity = [Because performance rules are necessary to provide guidance and support for maximizing performance and happiness]
Unit of analysis = [Ultimate Person (UP)]
Time deadline = [No time deadline (i.e. infinity)]
Success measure = [Maximum performance and maximum happiness from each UP]
Supplemental definitions = [There are two types of performance rules: individual performance rules and group performance rules]

The UW Level 8 Hypotheses

UPPP Hypotheses

Hypothesis ID# = [HUPSU8.1]
HUPSU8.1 Establishing and maintaining Define Problem as Step 1 of the UPPP is a necessary action because Define Problem is a necessary first step of maximizing performance and happiness.

Hypothesis ID# = [HUPSU8.2]
HUPSU8.2 Establishing and maintaining Define Solution (PSAs) as Step 2 of the UPPP is a necessary action because Define Solution (PSAs) is a necessary second step of maximizing performance and happiness.

Hypothesis ID# = [HUPSU8.3]
HUPSU8.3 Establishing and maintaining Perform Solution (PSAs) as Step 3 of the UPPP is a necessary action because Perform Solution (PSAs) is a necessary third step of maximizing performance and happiness.

Hypothesis ID# = [HUPSU8.4]
HUPSU8.4 Establishing and maintaining Evaluate Results as Step 4 of the UPPP is a necessary action because Evaluate Results is a necessary fourth step of maximizing performance and happiness.

Hypothesis ID# = [HUPSU8.5]
HUPSU8.5 Establishing and maintaining Repeat Steps 2-4 continuously on new solutions as Step 5 of the UPPP is a necessary action because Repeat Steps 2-4 continuously on new solutions is a necessary fifth step of maximizing performance and happiness.

Hypothesis ID# = [HUPSU8.6]
HUPSU8.6 Establishing and maintaining Perfect the UPPP and Have Fun as Step 4 of the UPPP is a necessary action because Perfect the UPPP and Have Fun is a necessary sixth step of maximizing performance and happiness.

Hypothesis ID# = [HUPSPR8.1]
HUPSPR8.1Establishing and maintaining Performance Rules is a necessary action because performance rules are necessary to provide guidance and support for maximizing performance and happiness.

THE PEOPLE

ULTIMATE PERSON SYSTEM

ULTIMATE PERSON PERFORMANCE PROCESS

STEP 1 DEFINE PROBLEM	UPSU8.1
STEP 2 DEFINE SOLUTION	UPSU8.2
STEP 3 PERFORM SOLUTION	UPSU8.3
STEP 4 EVALUATE RESULTS	UPSU8.4
STEP 5 REPEAT STEPS 2-4	UPSU8.5
STEP 6 PERFECT UPPP	UPSU8.6
PERFORMANCE RULES	UPSPR8.1

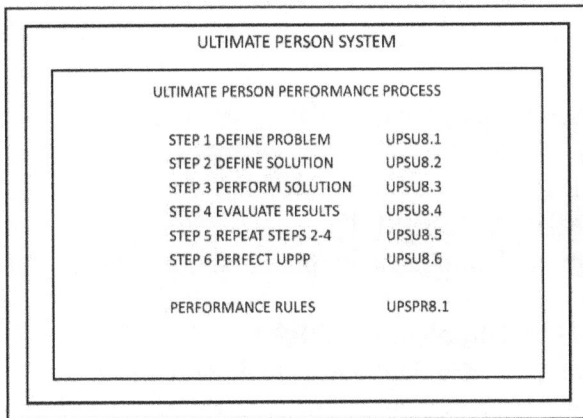

UW LEVEL 8 DIAGRAM

The UW Level 8 diagram illustrates the six steps of the UPPP: Step 1 Define problem ID# = UPSU8.1; Step 2 Define solution (PSAs) ID# = UPSU8.2; Step 3 Perform solution (PSAs) ID# = UPSU8.3; Step 4 Evaluate results ID# = UPSU8.4; Repeat steps 2-4 continuously on new solutions ID# = UPSU8.5; Perfect the UPPP and have fun ID# = UPSU8.6 and Performance Rules ID# = UPSPR8.1.

The UW Level 9 Scientific Solution

The UW Level 9 solution is defined by first sub-dividing the Level 8 problems into the Level 9 sub-problems. Then the UW scientific method is used to formulate the Level 9 characterizations and Level 9 hypotheses. The Level 9 hypotheses serve as the Level 9 scientific solution. Here are the steps involved:

Step 1 – Problem UPSPR8.1 performance rules is subdivided into two sub-problems: individual performance rules UPSPR9.1; and group performance rules UPSPR9.2

Step 2 – The Level 9 characterizations and hypotheses are defined as follows:
The UW Level 9 Characterizations

Performance Rules Elements

Characterization ID# = [CUPSPR9.1]
PSA ID# = [PSA UPSPR9.1]
PSA name = [Establish and maintain individual performance rules]
Problem ID# = [Problem UPSPR9.1]
Problem name [Individual performance rules]
Action name = [Establish and maintain]
Reason for necessity = [Because individual performance rules are necessary to provide guidance to individual UPs for performing the four steps of the UPPP]
Unit of analysis = [Ultimate Person (UP)]

Time deadline = [No time deadline (i.e. infinity)]
Success measure = [Maximum performance and maximum happiness for each UP]
Supplemental definitions = [There are four individual performance rules: 1) clearly identify PSAs; 2) get feedback on progress; 3) maintain challenge/skill balance; and 4) maintain safety awareness]

Characterization ID# = [CUPSPR9.2]
PSA ID# = [PSA UPSPR9.2]
PSA name = [Establish and maintain group performance rules]
Problem ID# = [Problem UPSPR9.2]
Problem name [Group performance rules]
Action name = [Establish and maintain]
Reason for necessity = [Because group performance rules are necessary to provide guidance to groups of UPs for performing the four steps of the UPPP]
Unit of analysis = [Ultimate Person (UP)]
Time deadline = [No time deadline (i.e. infinity)]
Success Measure = [Maximum performance and maximum happiness for each group of UPs]
Supplemental definitions = [There are four group performance rules: 1) apply the four individual performance rules to the group; 2) utilize a best practices democracy; 3) localize your activity, and 4) communicate with credibility]

The UW Level 9 Hypotheses

Performance Rules Hypotheses

Hypothesis ID# = [HUPSPR9.1]
HUPSPR9.2 Establishing and maintaining individual performance rules is a necessary action because individual performance rules are necessary to provide guidance to individual UPs for performing the four steps of the UPPP.

Hypothesis ID# = [HUPSPR9.2]
HUPSPR9.2 Establishing and maintaining group performance rules is a necessary action because group performance rules are necessary to provide guidance to groups of UPs for performing the four steps of the UPPP.

THE PEOPLE

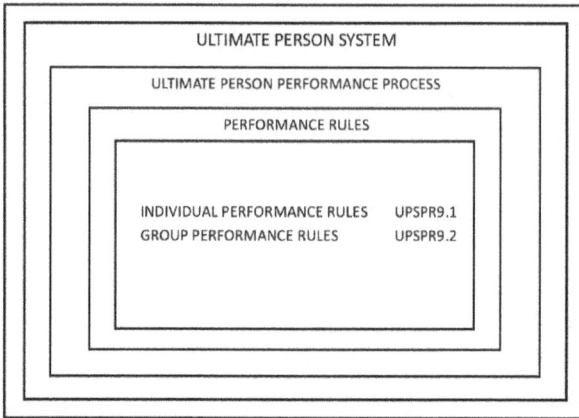

ULTIMATE PERSON SYSTEM

ULTIMATE PERSON PERFORMANCE PROCESS

PERFORMANCE RULES

INDIVIDUAL PERFORMANCE RULES   UPSPR9.1
GROUP PERFORMANCE RULES   UPSPR9.2

UW LEVEL 9 DIAGRAM

The UW Level 9 diagram illustrates the two types of performance rules: individual performance rules ID# = UPSPR9.1; and group performance rules ID# = UPSPR9.2.

The UW Level 10 Scientific Solution

The UW Level 10 solution is defined by first sub-dividing the Level 9 problems into the Level 10 sub-problems. Then the UW scientific method is used to formulate the Level 10 characterizations and Level 10 hypotheses. The Level 10 hypotheses serve as the Level 10 scientific solution. Here are the steps involved:

Step 1 – Problem UPSPR9.1 individual performance rules is sub-divided into individual performance rules Elements: clearly identify PSAs UPSPRI10.1; get feedback on progress UPSPRI10.2; maintain challenge/skill balance UPSPRI10.3; and maintain safety awareness UPSPRI10.4. Problem UPSPR9.2 group performance rules is sub-divided into group performance rules elements: apply the four individual performance rules to the group UPSPRG10.1; utilize a best practices democracy UPSPRG10.2; localize your activity UPSPRG10.3; and communicate with credibility UPSPRG10.4

Step 2 – The Level 10 characterizations and hypotheses are defined as follows:

The UW Level 10 Characterizations

Individual Performance Rules Elements

Characterization ID# = [CUPSPRI10.1]
PSA ID# = [PSA UPSPRI10.1]
PSA name = [Establish and maintain the performance rule of Clearly Identify PSAs]
Problem ID# = [Problem UPSPRI10.1]
Problem name [Clearly identify PSAs]
Action name = [Establish and maintain]
Reason for necessity = [Because clearly identified PSAs is a condition of achieving Flow during PSA performance]
Unit of analysis = [Ultimate Person (UP)]
Time deadline = [No time deadline (i.e. infinity)]
Success measure = [Correctly identified PSAs]
Supplemental definitions = [Correctly identify PSAs – PSAs that when performed the first time, actually solve the problem]

Characterization ID# = [CUPSPRI10.2]
PSA ID# = [PSA UPSPRI10.2]

PSA name = [Establish and maintain the performance rule of Get Feedback on Progress]
Problem ID# = [Problem UPSPRI10.2]
Problem name [Get feedback on progress]
Action name = [Establish and maintain]
Reason for necessity = [Because feedback on progress is a condition of achieving Flow during PSA performance]
Unit of analysis = [Ultimate Person (UP)]
Time deadline = [No time deadline (i.e. infinity)]
Success measure = [Continuous, immediate feedback on progress]

Characterization ID# = [CUPSPRI10.3]
PSA ID# = [PSA UPSPRI10.3]
PSA name = [Establish and maintain the performance rule of Maintain a Challenge/Skill Balance]
Problem ID# = [Problem UPSPRI10.3]
Problem name [Maintain Challenge/Skill Balance]
Action name = [Establish and maintain]
Reason for necessity = [Because the Challenge/Skill Balance is a condition of achieving Flow during PSA performance]
Unit of analysis = [Ultimate Person (UP)]
Time deadline = [No time deadline (i.e. infinity)]
Success measure = [Highly focused attention on PSAs, and personal confidence and enjoyment while performing them]

Characterization ID# = [CUPSPRI10.4]
PSA ID# = [PSA UPSPRI10.4]
PSA name = [Establish and maintain the performance rule of Maintain Safety Awareness]
Problem ID# = [Problem UPSPRI10.4]
Problem name [Maintain safety awareness]
Action name = [Establish and maintain]
Reason for necessity = [Because safety awareness is necessary to ensure that UPs can respond to safety hazards]
Unit of analysis = [Ultimate Person (UP)]
Time deadline = [No time deadline (i.e. infinity)]

Success measure = [Responsiveness to safety hazards]

Group Performance Rules Elements

Characterization ID# = [CUPSPRG10.1]
PSA ID# = [PSA UPSPRG10.1]
PSA name = [Establish and maintain the group performance rule of Apply the Four Individual Performance Rules to The Group]
Problem ID# = [Problem UPSPRG10.1]
Problem name [Apply the four individual performance rules to the group]
Action name = [Establish and maintain]
Reason for necessity = [Because the four individual performance rules are necessary for groups to sustain group Flow]
Unit of analysis = [Ultimate Person (UP)]
Time deadline = [No time deadline (i.e. infinity)]
Success measure = [Maximum group performance and happiness]

Characterization ID# = [CUPSPRG10.2]
PSA ID# = [PSA UPSPRG10.2]
PSA name = [Establish and maintain the group performance rule of Utilize a Best Practices Democracy]
Problem ID# = [Problem UPSPRG10.2]
Problem name [Utilize a best practices democracy]
Action name = [Establish and maintain]
Reason for necessity = [Because the basic tenants of a democracy are necessary to maximize group performance and happiness]
Unit of analysis = [Ultimate Person (UP)]
Time deadline = [No time deadline (i.e. infinity)]
Success Measure = [Maximum group performance and happiness]
Supplemental Definitions = [Basic tenants of a democracy = free speech, equal opportunity, fair competition and rule of law].

Characterization ID# = [CUPSPRG10.3]
PSA ID# = [PSA UPSPRG10.3]

PSA name = [Establish and maintain the group performance rule of Localize Your Activity]
Problem ID# = [Problem UPSPRG10.3]
Problem name [Localize your activity]
Action name = [Establish and maintain]
Reason for necessity = [Because localizing your activity is necessary to ensure that local laws and business practices are adhered to]
Unit of analysis = [Ultimate Person (UP)]
Time deadline = [No time deadline (i.e. infinity)]
Success measure = [All local laws and business practices are followed]

Characterization ID# = [CUPSPRG10.4]
PSA ID# = [PSA UPSPRG10.4]
PSA name = [Establish and maintain the group performance rule of Communicate with Credibility]
Problem ID# = [Problem UPSPRG10.4]
Problem name [Communicate with credibility]
Action name = [Establish and maintain]
Reason for necessity = [Because credible communication is accurate, reliable, objective, testable, and relevant communication between UPs]
Unit of analysis = [Ultimate Person (UP)]
Time deadline = [No time deadline (i.e. infinity)]
Success measure = [Accurate, reliable, objective, testable, and relevant communication between UPs]
Supplemental Definitions = [UW Experiment Form = a form to ensure credible communication]

The UW Level 10 Hypotheses

Individual Performance Rules Hypotheses

Hypothesis ID# = [HUPSPRI10.1]
HUPSPRI10.1 Establishing and maintaining the performance rule of Clearly Identify PSAs is a necessary action because the

clearly identified PSAs are a condition of achieving Flow during PSA performance.

Hypothesis ID# = [HUPSPRI10.2]
HUPSPRI10.2 Establishing and maintaining the performance rule of Get Feedback on Progress is a necessary action because feedback on progress is a condition of achieving Flow during PSA performance.

Hypothesis ID# = [HUPSPRI10.3]
HUPSPRI10.3 Establishing and maintaining the performance rule of Maintain Challenge/Skill Balance is a necessary action because a challenge/skill balance is a condition of achieving Flow during PSA performance.

Hypothesis ID# = [HUPSPRI10.4]
HUPSPRI10.4 Establishing and maintaining the performance rule of Maintain Safety Awareness is a necessary action because safety awareness is necessary to respond to safety hazards.

Group Performance Rules Hypotheses

Hypothesis ID# = [HUPSPRG10.1]
HUPSPRG10.1 Establishing and maintaining the group performance rule of Apply the Four Individual Performance Rules to The Group is a necessary action because the four individual performance rules are necessary for groups to sustain Group Flow.

Hypothesis ID# = [HUPSPRG10.2]
HUPSPRG10.2 Establishing and maintaining the group performance rule of Utilize a Best Practices Democracy is a necessary action because the basic tenants of a democracy are necessary to maximize group performance and happiness.

Hypothesis ID# = [HUPSPRG10.3]

HUPSPRG10.3 Establishing and maintaining the group performance rule of Localize Your Activity is a necessary action to ensure that local laws and business practices are adhered to.

Hypothesis ID# = [HUPSPRG10.4]
UPSPRG10.4 Establishing and maintaining the group performance rule of Communicate with Credibility is a necessary action because credible communication is accurate, reliable, objective, testable, and relevant communication between UPs.

THE PEOPLE

ULTIMATE PERSON SYSTEM

ULTIMATE PERSON PERFORMANCE PROCESS

PERFORMANCE RULES

IND. PERFORMANCE RULES   GROUP PERFORMANCE RULES

1) CLEARLY ID PSAs UPSPRI10.1   1) APPLY 4 IND RULES UPSPRG10.1
2) GET FEEDBACK UPSPRI10.2   2) BP DEMOCRACY UPSPRG10.2
3) C/S BALANCE UPSPRI10.3   3) LOCALIZE ACTIVITY UPSPRG10.3
4) SAFETY AWARE UPSPRI10.4   4) COMM. CREDIBILITY UPSPRG10.4

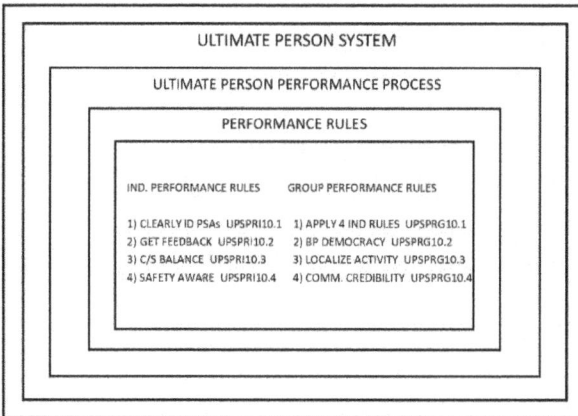

UW LEVEL 10 DIAGRAM

The UW Level 10 diagram illustrates the identities of the individual performance rules and the group performance rules. The individual performance rules are: 1) clearly identify PSAs ID# = UPSPRI10.1; 2) get feedback on progress ID# = UPSPRI10.2; 3) maintain challenge/skill balance ID# = UPSPRI10.3; and 4) maintain safety awareness ID# = UPSPRI10.4. The group performance rules are: 1) apply the four individual performance rules to groups ID# = UPSPRG10.1; 2) utilize a best practices democracy ID# = UPSPRG10.2; 3) localize your activity ID# = UPSPRG10.3; and 4) communicate with credibility ID# = UPSPRG10.4.

4

SUMMARY OF THE ULTIMATE WORLD HYPOTHESES

Hypotheses are theoretical explanations of the characterizations (i.e. definitions and measurements) of a scientific study. An individual hypothesis, or set of hypotheses, is the actual "theory" of the study. So the set of UW Hypotheses listed below is the actual UW Theory as mentioned in the introduction of this book. The purpose of this chapter is to provide a summarized version of the UW Theory. Two different versions of the theory are provided – a list version, and a diagram version.

The basic theoretical explanation of each UW hypothesis is that a certain PSA is necessary for human survival (i.e. "do or die" for the world) because of its Reason for Necessity. All UW hypotheses are linked together in a hierarchical fashion with the super problem of human survival at the top level of the hierarchy. The Reasons for Necessity provide the logical coherence with the PSA hierarchy.

The Complete List of UW Hypotheses

There are a total of 70 hypotheses in the initial edition of UW Theory. This includes the three hypotheses of the UW Context which are listed first. The remaining 67 hypotheses are then listed from the top level down.

The Three Hypotheses of the UW Context

Hypothesis ID# = [HC1]
HC1 Establishing and maintaining the human survival issue as the most important issue is a necessary action because it is common sense to do so, and because human extinction would be the most catastrophic event imaginable to humans.

Hypothesis ID# = [HC2]
HC2 Establishing and maintaining a problem solving approach to the human survival issue based on maximum problem solving skill over time is a necessary action because it resolves the maximum complexity of the human survival problem imposed by the universe.

Hypothesis ID# = [HC3]
HC3 Establishing and maintaining a scientific solution to the human survival problem is a necessary action because a scientific solution is accurate, reliable, objective and testable.

The Top Level Hypothesis (i.e. The Supreme Hypothesis)

Hypothesis ID# = [H1.0]
H1.0 Establishing and maintaining UP_{MAX} is a necessary action because of the maximum problem complexity of the human survival problem, which requires maximum problem solving skill over time to resolve this maximum problem complexity.

Note – the short form of The Supreme Hypothesis is:

$$UW = UP_{MAX}$$

Level 2 Hypotheses

Hypothesis ID# = [H2.1]
H2.1 Establishing and maintaining UPs for all safe locations in the universe is a necessary action because locations in the universe (including planet earth) are not permanently safe for human habitation.

Hypothesis ID# = [H2.2]
H2.2 Establishing and maintaining maximum group UP problem solving performance is a necessary action because maximum group UP problem solving performance is required for solving complex survival problems over time.

Hypothesis ID# = [H2.3]
H2.3 Establishing and maintaining UPs for all time is a necessary action because individual UPs do not have permanent lifetimes.

Level 3 Hypotheses

Hypothesis ID# = [H3.1]
H3.1 Establishing and maintaining the Human Survival Problem Solver is a necessary action because a world-wide computer based solutions manager is necessary to manage all human survival problems in all safe locations of the universe and all time.

Hypothesis ID# = [H3.2]
H3.2 Establishing and maintaining the Ultimate World is a necessary action because a world-wide group of UPs that work together as a team is necessary to maximize group problem solving skill over time.

Hypothesis ID# = [H3.3]
H3.3 Establishing and maintaining a Control Theory Framework for integrating the HSPS and UW is a necessary action because control theory facilitates maximum use of feedback between HSPS and UW to correct mistakes, adapt to change, deal with unknowns, maintain UW stability, and maximize performance improvement over time.

CONTROL THEORY FRAMEWORK

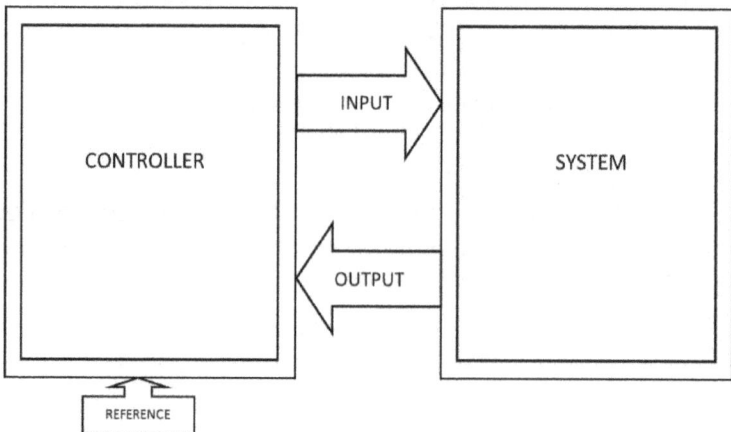

The Control Theory Framework diagram (Hypothesis 3.3) illustrates the framework of the five elements of a control system: the reference, the controller, the input, the output and the system.

ULTIMATE WORLD THEORY

THE TECHNOLOGY   **THE PEOPLE**

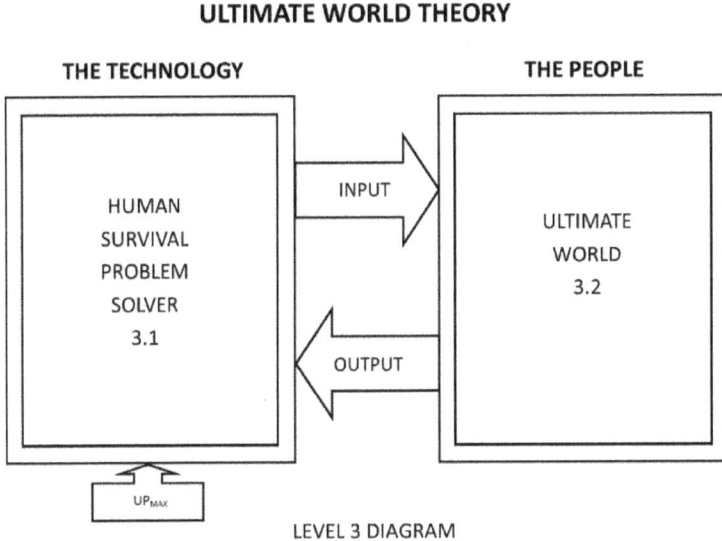

LEVEL 3 DIAGRAM

The Level 3 diagram illustrates how the Ultimate World (UW) and the Human Survival Problem Solver (HSPS) are integrated within the control theory framework. The UW (Hypothesis 3.2) is the system and HSPS (Hypothesis 3.1) is the controller.

IMPORTANT NOTE: Starting with Level 4, the UW Hypotheses (i.e. the people issues) are separated from the HSPS Hypotheses (i.e. the technology issues). The people issues are separated so that they can be given special attention. The Level 4 UW Hypotheses will start on page 123, and the Level 4 HSPS Hypotheses will continue here.

The HSPS Level 4 Hypotheses

HSPS Hypotheses

Hypothesis ID# = [HHC4.1]
HHC4.1 Establishing and maintaining a controller within HSPS is a necessary action because a controller is a necessary element of control theory.

Hypothesis ID# = [HHR4.1]
HHR4.1 Establishing and maintaining a reference within HSPS is a necessary action because a reference is a necessary element of control theory.

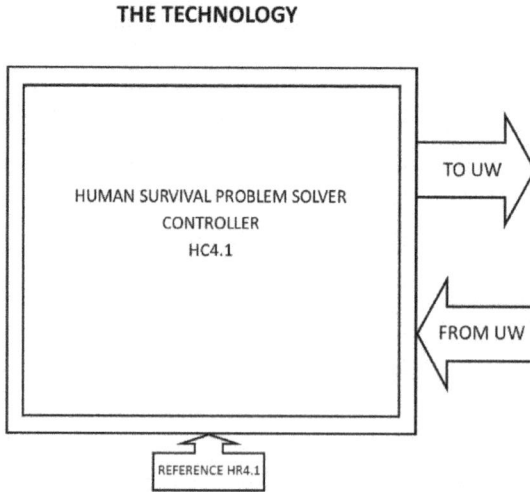

THE TECHNOLOGY

HUMAN SURVIVAL PROBLEM SOLVER
CONTROLLER
HC4.1

TO UW

FROM UW

REFERENCE HR4.1

HSPS LEVEL 4 DIAGRAM

The HSPS Level 4 diagram illustrates the two primary elements of the HSPS: the controller and the reference. Note that all HSPS elements have an "H" prefix on their identification numbers. Also note that the additional "H" prefix stands for "Hypothesis." For example, the HSPS controller hypothesis has the following identification number "HHC4.1".

The HSPS Level 5 Hypotheses

Controller Hypotheses

Hypothesis ID# = [HHC5.1]
HHC5.1 Establishing and maintaining a HSPS expert system is a necessary action because an expert system is necessary to manage the specialized sub-problems of UP_{MAX} in a computer-based, safe, intelligent fashion.

Hypothesis ID# = [HHC5.2]
HHC5.2 Establishing and maintaining a HSPS application set is a necessary action because an application set is necessary to identify and perform specific solutions to specific problem types within the human survival problem.

Reference Hypotheses

Hypothesis ID# = [HHR5.1]
HHR5.1 Establishing and maintaining UP_{MAX} as the HSPS reference is a necessary action because UP_{MAX} is the desired output of the UW.

THE TECHNOLOGY

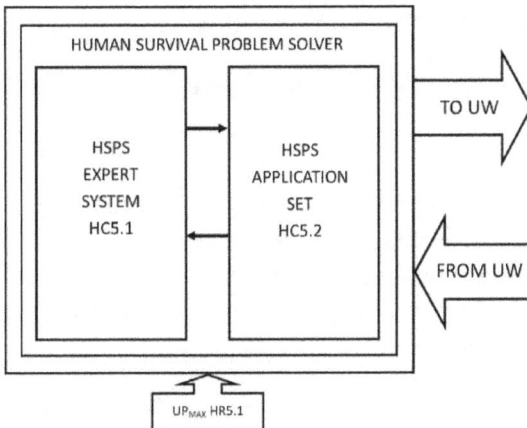

HSPS LEVEL 5 DIAGRAM

The HSPS Level 5 diagram illustrates the two primary elements of the HSPS controller: the HSPS expert system and the HSPS application set. The HSPS expert system hypothesis is Hypothesis ID# = HHC5.1; and the HSPS application set hypothesis is Hypothesis ID# = HHC5.2. Plus the HSPS reference of UP_{MAX}. The HSPS reference hypothesis is Hypothesis ID# = HHR5.1.

The HSPS Level 6 Hypotheses

HSPS Expert System Hypotheses

Hypothesis ID# = [HHES6.1]
HHES6.1 Establishing and maintaining an HSPS knowledge base is a necessary action because a knowledge base is a necessary element of an expert system.

Hypothesis ID# = [HHES6.2]
HHES6.2 Establishing and maintaining an HSPS inference engine is a necessary action because an inference engine is a necessary element of an expert system.

Hypothesis ID# = [HHES6.3]
HHES6.3 Establishing and maintaining an HSPS user interface is a necessary action because a user interface is a necessary element of an expert system.

HSPS Application Set Hypotheses

Hypothesis ID# = [HHAS6.1]
HHAS6.1 Establishing and maintaining a UW Theory Education application is a necessary action because a UW Theory education application is necessary to maximize problem solving skill on the problem of educating the world on UW Theory and certifying everyone as UPs.

Hypothesis ID# = [HHAS6.2]
HHAS6.2 Establishing and maintaining a Human Survival Problem Identification application is a necessary action because a human survival problem identification application is necessary to maximize problem solving skill on the problem of identifying human survival threats.

Hypothesis ID# = [HHAS6.3]
HHAS6.3 Establishing and maintaining a Space Life Economy application is a necessary action because a space life economy application is necessary to maximize problem solving skill on the problem of managing a space-based economy.

Hypothesis ID# = [HHAS6.4]
HHAS6.4 Establishing and maintaining a Safety Awareness application is a necessary action because a safety awareness application is necessary to maximize problem solving skill on the problem of safety awareness in all PSAs.

THE TECHNOLOGY

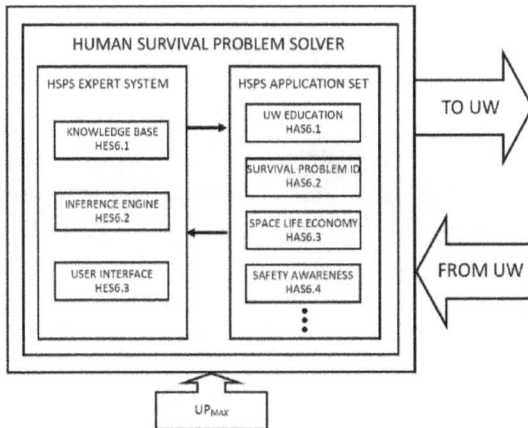

HSPS LEVEL 6 DIAGRAM

The HSPS Level 6 diagram illustrates the detailed elements within the HSPS expert system and the HSPS application set. The knowledge base hypothesis is Hypothesis ID# = HHES6.1. The inference engine hypothesis is Hypothesis ID# = HHES6.2. The user interface hypothesis is Hypothesis ID# = HHES6.3. The UW Theory education application hypothesis is Hypothesis ID# = HHAS6.1. The survival threat ID application hypothesis is Hypothesis ID# = HHAS6.2. The space life economy application hypothesis is Hypothesis ID# = HHAS6.3. The safety awareness application hypothesis is Hypothesis ID# = HHAS6.4.

The HSPS Level 7 Hypotheses

Knowledge Base Hypotheses

Hypothesis ID# = [HHKB7.1]
HHKB7.1 Establishing and maintaining a definitional knowledge base is a necessary action because a definition knowledge base is necessary to manage PSA definitions for all applications.

Hypothesis ID# = [HHKB7.2]
HHKB7.2 Establishing and maintaining a performance knowledge base is a necessary action because a performance knowledge base is necessary to manage PSA performance knowledge in a way that maximizes user performance and user happiness for all applications.

THE TECHNOLOGY

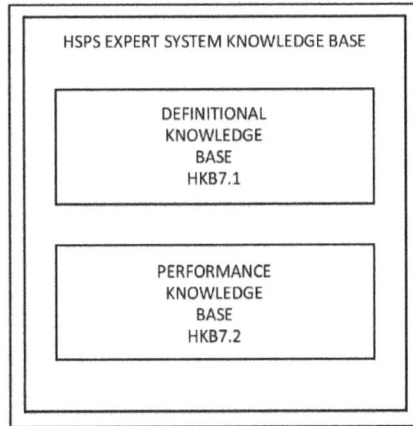

```
┌─────────────────────────────────────────┐
│  HSPS EXPERT SYSTEM KNOWLEDGE BASE        │
│                                           │
│   ┌───────────────────────────────────┐  │
│   │         DEFINITIONAL              │  │
│   │         KNOWLEDGE                 │  │
│   │         BASE                      │  │
│   │         HKB7.1                    │  │
│   └───────────────────────────────────┘  │
│                                           │
│   ┌───────────────────────────────────┐  │
│   │         PERFORMANCE               │  │
│   │         KNOWLEDGE                 │  │
│   │         BASE                      │  │
│   │         HKB7.2                    │  │
│   └───────────────────────────────────┘  │
│                                           │
└─────────────────────────────────────────┘
```

HSPS LEVEL 7 DIAGRAM 1

The HSPS Level 7 diagram 1 illustrates the two knowledge bases within the HSPS expert system knowledge base. The definitional knowledge base hypothesis is Hypothesis ID# = HHKB7.1. The performance knowledge base hypothesis is Hypothesis ID# = HHKB7.2.

Inference Engine Hypotheses

Hypothesis ID# = [HHIE7.1]
HHIE7.1 Establishing and maintaining a definitional inference rule is a necessary action because a definitional inference rule is necessary to manage the interaction between the users and the definitional knowledge base in a necessitive fashion.

Hypothesis ID# = [HHIE7.2]
HHIE7.2 Establishing and maintaining a performance inference rule is a necessary action because a performance inference rule is necessary to manage the interaction between the users and the performance knowledge base in a necessitive fashion.

THE TECHNOLOGY

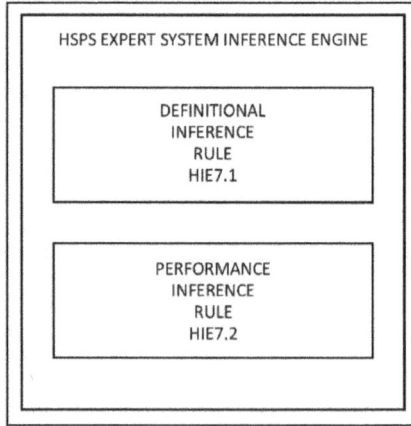

```
┌─────────────────────────────────────────────┐
│  HSPS EXPERT SYSTEM INFERENCE ENGINE          │
│                                               │
│   ┌───────────────────────────────────────┐  │
│   │            DEFINITIONAL                │  │
│   │             INFERENCE                  │  │
│   │               RULE                     │  │
│   │              HIE7.1                    │  │
│   └───────────────────────────────────────┘  │
│                                               │
│   ┌───────────────────────────────────────┐  │
│   │            PERFORMANCE                 │  │
│   │             INFERENCE                  │  │
│   │               RULE                     │  │
│   │              HIE7.2                    │  │
│   └───────────────────────────────────────┘  │
│                                               │
└─────────────────────────────────────────────┘
```

HSPS LEVEL 7 DIAGRAM 2

The HSPS Level 7 diagram 2 illustrates the two elements of the HSPS expert system inference engine. The definitional inference rule hypothesis is Hypothesis ID# = HHIE7.1. The performance inference rule hypothesis is Hypothesis ID# = HHIE7.2

User Interface Hypotheses

Hypothesis ID# = [HHUI7.1]
HHUI7.1 Establishing and maintaining a user input/output section of the user interface is a necessary action because a user input/output is necessary to facilitate user input and output from HSPS.

Hypothesis ID# = [HHUI7.2]
HHUI7.2 Establishing and maintaining a PSA list section of the user interface is a necessary action because a PSA list is necessary to manage the PSAs that the user will be performing.

Hypothesis ID# = [HHUI7.3]
HHUI7.3 Establishing and maintaining a support section of the user interface is a necessary action because support is necessary to assist users in maximizing performance on their PSA list.

THE TECHNOLOGY

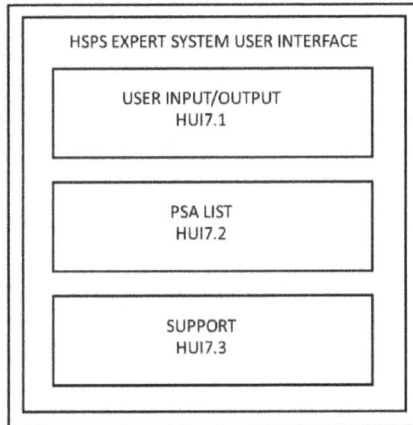

```
┌─────────────────────────────────────────┐
│ ┌───────────────────────────────────┐   │
│ │ HSPS EXPERT SYSTEM USER INTERFACE  │   │
│ │ ┌─────────────────────────────┐   │   │
│ │ │     USER INPUT/OUTPUT        │   │   │
│ │ │        HUI7.1                │   │   │
│ │ └─────────────────────────────┘   │   │
│ │ ┌─────────────────────────────┐   │   │
│ │ │        PSA LIST              │   │   │
│ │ │        HUI7.2                │   │   │
│ │ └─────────────────────────────┘   │   │
│ │ ┌─────────────────────────────┐   │   │
│ │ │        SUPPORT               │   │   │
│ │ │        HUI7.3                │   │   │
│ │ └─────────────────────────────┘   │   │
│ └───────────────────────────────────┘   │
└─────────────────────────────────────────┘
```

HSPS LEVEL 7 DIAGRAM 3

The HSPS Level 7 diagram 3 illustrates the three elements of the HSPS expert system user interface. The user input/output hypothesis is Hypothesis ID# = HHUI7.1. The PSA list hypothesis is Hypothesis ID# = HHUI7.2. The support hypothesis is Hypothesis ID# = HHUI7.3.

UW Theory Education Application Hypotheses

UW Theory Online Course Hypothesis

HHAS7.1 Establishing and maintaining a UW Theory online course is a necessary action because a UW Theory online course is a necessary to educate and certify UPs as experts on UW Theory.

UP Skill Online Course Hypothesis

HHAS7.2 Establishing and maintaining a UP Skill online course is a necessary action because a UP Skill online course is necessary to educate everyone in the world on UP Skill and certify everyone as UPs.

THE TECHNOLOGY

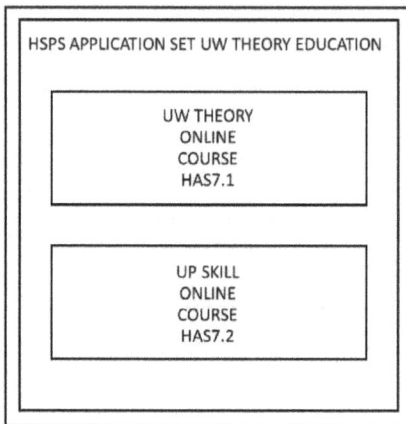

```
┌──────────────────────────────────────────────┐
│ ┌──────────────────────────────────────────┐ │
│ │ HSPS APPLICATION SET UW THEORY EDUCATION   │ │
│ │                                            │ │
│ │   ┌────────────────────────────────────┐   │ │
│ │   │           UW THEORY                │   │ │
│ │   │           ONLINE                   │   │ │
│ │   │           COURSE                   │   │ │
│ │   │           HAS7.1                   │   │ │
│ │   └────────────────────────────────────┘   │ │
│ │                                            │ │
│ │   ┌────────────────────────────────────┐   │ │
│ │   │           UP SKILL                 │   │ │
│ │   │           ONLINE                   │   │ │
│ │   │           COURSE                   │   │ │
│ │   │           HAS7.2                   │   │ │
│ │   └────────────────────────────────────┘   │ │
│ │                                            │ │
│ └──────────────────────────────────────────┘ │
└──────────────────────────────────────────────┘
```

HSPS LEVEL 7 DIAGRAM 4

The HSPS Level 7 diagram 4 illustrates the two UW Theory education courses. The UW Theory online course hypothesis is Hypothesis ID# = HHAS7.1 and the UP Skill online course hypothesis is Hypothesis ID# = HHAS7.2. Both of these online courses are now available!

IMPORTANT NOTE: The next section on the UW Hypotheses is separate from the HSPS Hypotheses. The UW Hypotheses start at Level 4.

The UW Level 4 Hypotheses

UW Control System Elements

Hypothesis ID# = [HUR4.1]
HUR4.1 Establishing and maintaining a reference for the
UW is a necessary action because a reference is a necessary
element of control theory.

Hypothesis ID# = [HUC4.1]
HUC4.1 Establishing and maintaining a controller for the
UW is a necessary action because a controller is a necessary
element of control theory.

Hypothesis ID# = [HUI4.1]
HUI4.1 Establishing and maintaining an input to the UW is
a necessary action because a system input is a necessary element of control theory.

Hypothesis ID# = [HUO4.1]
HUO4.1 Establishing and maintaining an output from the
UW is a necessary action because a system output is a nec-
essary element of control theory.

Hypothesis ID# = [HUS4.1]
HUS4.1 Establishing and maintaining a system within the
UW is a necessary action because a system is a necessary el-
ement of control theory.

THE PEOPLE

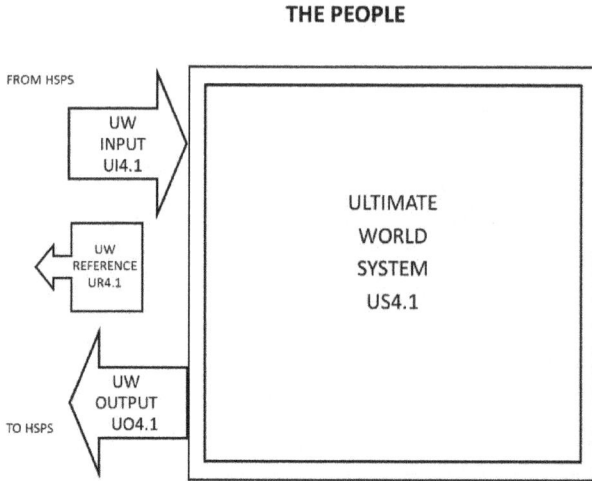

FROM HSPS

UW
INPUT
UI4.1

UW
REFERENCE
UR4.1

UW
OUTPUT
UO4.1

TO HSPS

ULTIMATE
WORLD
SYSTEM
US4.1

UW LEVEL 4 DIAGRAM

The UW Level 4 Diagram illustrates the five elements of the UW control system. The UW reference hypothesis is Hypothesis ID# = HUR4.1. The UW input hypothesis is Hypothesis ID# = HUI4.1. The UW output hypothesis is Hypothesis ID# = HUO4.1. The UW system hypothesis is Hypothesis ID# = HUS4.1. Note that the UW controller is the HSPS which is detailed earlier in this chapter.

The UW Level 5 Hypotheses

UW Reference Hypothesis

Hypothesis ID# = [HUR5.1]
HUR5.1 Establishing and maintaining UP_{MAX} as the UW reference is a necessary action because UP_{MAX} is the desired output of the UW system.

UW Controller Hypothesis

Hypothesis ID# = [HUC5.1]
HUC5.1 Establishing and maintaining HSPS as the controller of the UW is a necessary action because the HSPS is the primary controller within UW Theory.

UW Input Hypotheses

Hypothesis ID# = [HUI5.1]
HUI5.1 Establishing and maintaining new PSAs as a UW Input is a necessary action because new PSAs are necessary for solving new problems, and new problems are an on-going issue in the UW.

Hypothesis ID# = [HUI5.2]
HUI5.2 Establishing and maintaining paychecks as a UW Input is a necessary action because paychecks are a necessary exchange from the HSPS to the UPs for the UPs successful completion of PSAs.

Hypothesis ID# = [HUI5.3]
HUI5.3 Establishing and maintaining new non-UPs as a UW Input is a necessary action because new non-UP certified people are necessary achieve UP_{MAX}.

UW Output Hypotheses

Hypothesis ID# = [HUO5.1]
HUO5.1 Establishing and maintaining performance results as a UW Output is a necessary action because performance results are necessary feedback from the individual UPs on their performance on actual PSAs.

Hypothesis ID# = [HUO5.2]
HUO5.2 Establishing and maintaining UP_N as a UW Output is a necessary action because UP_N is necessary feedback to determine the progress of the UW.

UW System Hypothesis

Hypothesis ID# = [HPS5.1]
HPS5.1 Establishing and maintaining uniquely identified UPs from UP1 to UP_N as the UW System is a necessary action because uniquely identified UPs are necessary to ensure that each UP is performing PSAs in an optimal fashion, and is experiencing maximum paychecks and happiness.

THE PEOPLE

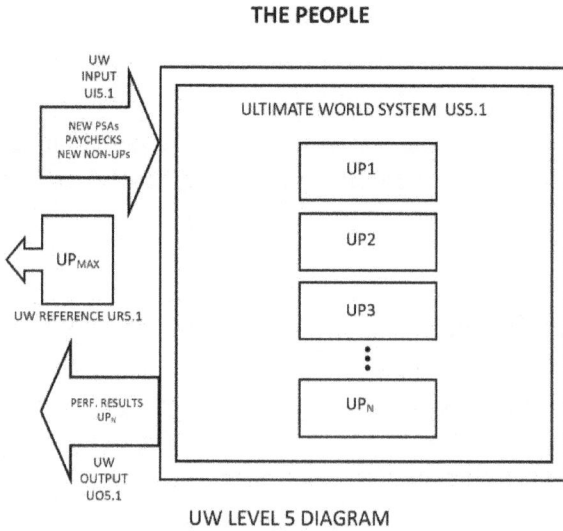

UW LEVEL 5 DIAGRAM

The UW Level 5 diagram identifies the five elements of the UW control system. The UW reference hypothesis (UP_{MAX}) is Hypothesis ID# = HUR5.1; the UW controller hypothesis (HSPS) is Hypothesis ID# = HUC5.1 (not pictured here); the UW input hypotheses (new PSAs, paychecks, new Non-UPs are Hypothesis ID# = HUI5.1-HUI5.3; the UW output hypotheses (performance results, UP_N) are Hypotheses ID# = HUO5.1-HUO5.2; and the UW system hypothesis ($UP1$-UP_N) is Hypothesis ID# = HUS5.1.

The UW Level 6 Hypotheses

The UP Control System Elements

Hypothesis ID# = [HUR6.1]
HUPR6.1 Establishing and maintaining a reference for each UP is a necessary action because a reference is a necessary element of control theory.

Hypothesis ID# = [HUPC6.1]
HUPC6.1 Establishing and maintaining a controller for each UP is a necessary action because a controller is a necessary element of control theory.

Hypothesis ID# = [HUPI6.1]
HUPI6.1 Establishing and maintaining an input for each UP is a necessary action because an input is a necessary element of control theory.

Hypothesis ID# = [HUPO6.1]
HUPO6.1 Establishing and maintaining an output for each UP is a necessary action because a output is a necessary element of control theory.

Hypothesis ID# = [HUPS6.1]
HUPS6.1 Establishing and maintaining a system for each UP is a necessary action because a system is a necessary element of control theory.

THE PEOPLE

```
FROM HSPS

         UP
       INPUT
       UPI6.1
                                ULTIMATE
         UP
      REFERENCE                  PERSON
       UPR6.1
                                 SYSTEM

                                 UPS6.1
         UP
       OUTPUT
       UPO6.1

TO HSPS
```

UW LEVEL 6 DIAGRAM

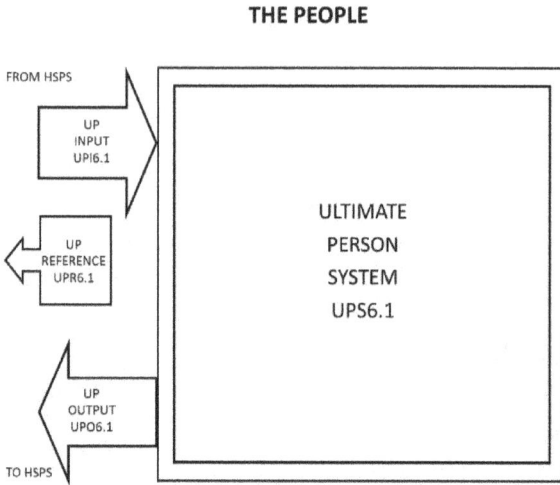

The UW Level 6 diagram illustrates the five elements of the UP control system. The UP reference hypothesis is Hypothesis ID# = HUPR6.1. The UP input hypothesis is Hypothesis ID# = HUPI6.1. The UP output hypothesis is Hypothesis ID# = HUPO6.1. The UP system hypothesis is Hypothesis ID# = HUPS6.1. Note that the UP controller is the HSPS, which is detailed earlier in this chapter.

The UW Level 7 Hypotheses

UP Reference Hypothesis

Hypothesis ID# = [HUPR7.1]
HUPR7.1 Establishing and maintaining maximum personal and professional problem solving skill as the UP reference is a necessary action because maximum personal and professional problem solving skill are the desired outputs of the UP system.

UP Controller Hypothesis

HUPC7.1 Establishing and maintaining HSPS as the controller for each UP is a necessary action because the HSPS is the primary controller for all of UW Theory.

UP Input Hypothesis

HUPI7.1 Establishing and maintaining new PSAs and paychecks as inputs to each UP is a necessary action because new PSAs and paychecks are necessary inputs for solving new problems, and solving new problems is an on-going issue for each UP.

UP Output Hypothesis

HUPO7.1 Establishing and maintaining personal and professional problem solving skill performance results as the UP output is a necessary action because personal and professional problem solving skill performance results are necessary feedback from the individual UPs on their performance on actual PSAs.

UP System Hypothesis

HUPS7.1 Establishing and maintaining the Ultimate Person Performance Process (UPPP) as the UP system is a necessary action because the UPPP is necessary to maximize the performance and happiness of each UP.

THE PEOPLE

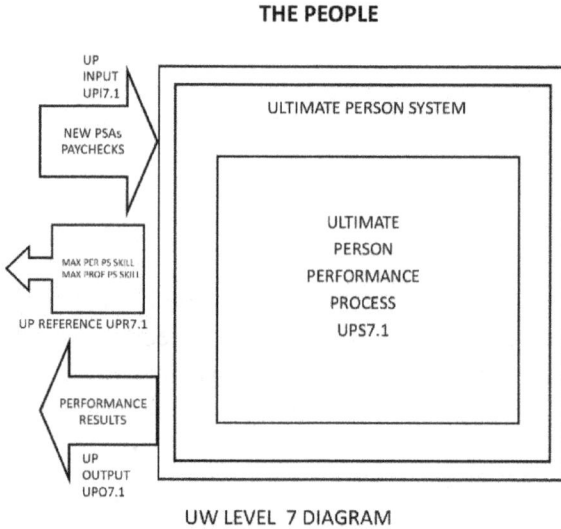

UW LEVEL 7 DIAGRAM

The UW Level 7 diagram illustrates the identities of each of the five elements of the UP control system. The UP reference hypothesis (maximum personal problem solving skill, maximum professional problem solving skill) is Hypothesis ID# = HUPR7.1; the UP controller hypothesis (HSPS) Hypothesis ID# = HUPC7.1; the UP input hypothesis (new PSAs, paychecks) is Hypothesis ID# = HUPI7.1; the UP output hypothesis (personal and professional problem solving skill performance results) is Hypothesis ID# = HUPO7.1; and the UP system hypothesis (UPPP) is Hypothesis ID# = HUPS7.1. And remember, the UP controller is the HSPS, which is detailed in Chapter 2.

The UW Level 8 Hypotheses

UPPP Hypotheses

Hypothesis ID# = [HUPSU8.1]
HUPSU8.1 Establishing and maintaining Define Problem as Step 1 of the UPPP is a necessary action because Define Problem is a necessary first step of maximizing performance and happiness.

Hypothesis ID# = [HUPSU8.2]
HUPSU8.2 Establishing and maintaining Define Solution (PSAs) as Step 2 of the UPPP is a necessary action because Define Solution (PSAs) is a necessary second step of maximizing performance and happiness.

Hypothesis ID# = [HUPSU8.3]
HUPSU8.3 Establishing and maintaining Perform Solution (PSAs) as Step 3 of the UPPP is a necessary action because Perform Solution (PSAs) is a necessary third step of maximizing performance and happiness.

Hypothesis ID# = [HUPSU8.4]
HUPSU8.4 Establishing and maintaining Evaluate Results as Step 4 of the UPPP is a necessary action because Evaluate Results is a necessary fourth step of maximizing performance and happiness.

Hypothesis ID# = [HUPSU8.5]
HUPSU8.5 Establishing and maintaining Repeat Steps 2-4 continuously on new solutions as Step 5 of the UPPP is a necessary action because Repeat Steps 2-4 continuously on new solutions is a necessary fifth step of maximizing performance and happiness.

Hypothesis ID# = [HUPSU8.6]
HUPSU8.6 Establishing and maintaining Perfect the UPPP and Have Fun as Step 4 of the UPPP is a necessary action because Perfect the UPPP and Have Fun is a necessary sixth step of maximizing performance and happiness.

Hypothesis ID# = [HUPSPR8.1]
HUPSPR8.1 Establishing and maintaining Performance Rules is a necessary action because performance rules are necessary to provide guidance and support for maximizing performance and happiness.

THE PEOPLE

```
┌─────────────────────────────────────────────┐
│ ┌─────────────────────────────────────────┐ │
│ │          ULTIMATE PERSON SYSTEM          │ │
│ │ ┌───────────────────────────────────────┐│ │
│ │ │  ULTIMATE PERSON PERFORMANCE PROCESS   ││ │
│ │ │                                       ││ │
│ │ │  STEP 1 DEFINE PROBLEM      UPSU8.1   ││ │
│ │ │  STEP 2 DEFINE SOLUTION     UPSU8.2   ││ │
│ │ │  STEP 3 PERFORM SOLUTION    UPSU8.3   ││ │
│ │ │  STEP 4 EVALUATE RESULTS    UPSU8.4   ││ │
│ │ │  STEP 5 REPEAT STEPS 2-4    UPSU8.5   ││ │
│ │ │  STEP 6 PERFECT UPPP        UPSU8.6   ││ │
│ │ │                                       ││ │
│ │ │  PERFORMANCE RULES          UPSPR8.1  ││ │
│ │ └───────────────────────────────────────┘│ │
│ └─────────────────────────────────────────┘ │
└─────────────────────────────────────────────┘
```

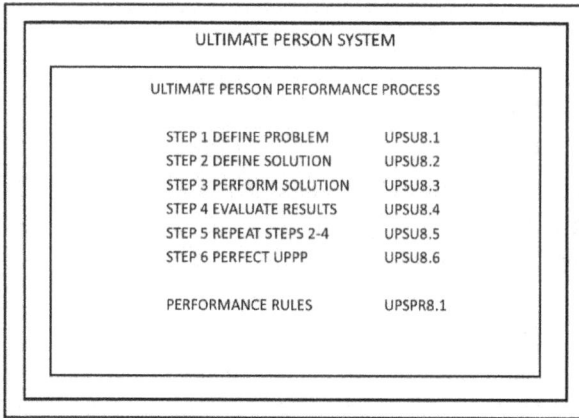

UW LEVEL 8 DIAGRAM

The UW Level 8 diagram illustrates the six steps of the UPPP and the performance rules. The UPPP Step 1 hypothesis (Define Problem) is Hypothesis ID# = HUPSU8.1. The UPPP Step 2 hypothesis (Define Solution) is Hypothesis ID# = HUPSU8.2. The UPPP Step 3 hypothesis (Perform Solution) is Hypothesis ID# = HUPSU8.3. The UPPP Step 4 hypothesis (Evaluate results) is Hypothesis ID# = HUPSU8.4. The UPPP Step 5 hypothesis (Repeat Steps 2-4 continuously) is Hypothesis ID# = HUPSU8.5. The UPPP Step 6 hypothesis (Perfect UPPP) is Hypothesis ID# = HUPSU8.6. And the Performance Rules prediction is Prediction ID# = HUPSPR8.1.

The UW Level 9 Hypotheses

Performance Rules Hypotheses

Hypothesis ID# = [HUPSPR9.1]
HUPSPR9.1 Establishing and maintaining individual performance rules is a necessary action because individual performance rules are necessary to provide guidance to individual UPs for performing the four steps of the UPPP.

Hypothesis ID# = [HUPSPR9.2]
HUPSPR9.2 Establishing and maintaining group performance rules is a necessary action because group performance rules are necessary to provide guidance to groups of UPs for performing the four steps of the UPPP.

THE PEOPLE

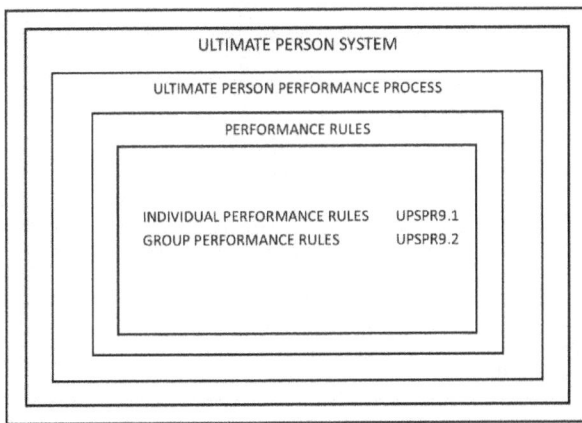

ULTIMATE PERSON SYSTEM

ULTIMATE PERSON PERFORMANCE PROCESS

PERFORMANCE RULES

INDIVIDUAL PERFORMANCE RULES	UPSPR9.1
GROUP PERFORMANCE RULES	UPSPR9.2

UW LEVEL 9 DIAGRAM

The UW Level 9 diagram illustrates the two types of performance rules. The individual performance rules Hypothesis ID# = HUPSPR9.1; and the group performance rules Hypothesis ID# = HUPSPR9.2.

The UW Level 10 Hypotheses

Individual Performance Rules Hypotheses

Hypothesis ID# = [HUPSPRI10.1]
HUPSPRI10.1 Establishing and maintaining the performance rule of Clearly Identify PSAs is a necessary action because the clearly identified PSAs are a condition of achieving Flow during PSA performance.

Hypothesis ID# = [HUPSPRI10.2]
HUPSPRI10.2 Establishing and maintaining the performance rule of Get Feedback on Progress is a necessary action because feedback on progress is a condition of achieving Flow during PSA performance.

Hypothesis ID# = [HUPSPRI10.3]
HUPSPRI10.3 Establishing and maintaining the performance rule of Maintain Challenge/Skill Balance is a necessary action because a challenge/skill balance is a condition of achieving Flow during PSA performance.

Hypothesis ID# = [HUPSPRI10.4]
HUPSPRI10.4 Establishing and maintaining the performance rule of Maintain Safety Awareness is a necessary action because safety awareness is necessary to respond to safety hazards.

Group Performance Rules Hypotheses

Hypothesis ID# = [HUPSPRG10.1]
HUPSPRG10.1 Establishing and maintaining the group performance rule of Apply the Four Individual Performance Rules to The Group is a necessary action because the four individual performance rules are necessary for groups to sustain Group Flow.

Hypothesis ID# = [HUPSPRG10.2]
HUPSPRG10.2 Establishing and maintaining the group performance rule of Utilize a Best Practices Democracy is a necessary action because the basic tenants of a democracy are necessary to maximize group performance and happiness.

Hypothesis ID# = [HUPSPRG10.3]
HUPSPRG10.3 Establishing and maintaining the group performance rule of Localize Your Activity is a necessary action to ensure that local laws and business practices are adhered to.

Hypothesis ID# = [HUPSPRG10.4]
HUPSPRG10.4 Establishing and maintaining the group performance rule of Communicate with Credibility is a necessary action because credible communication is accurate, reliable, objective, testable, and relevant communication between UPs.

THE PEOPLE

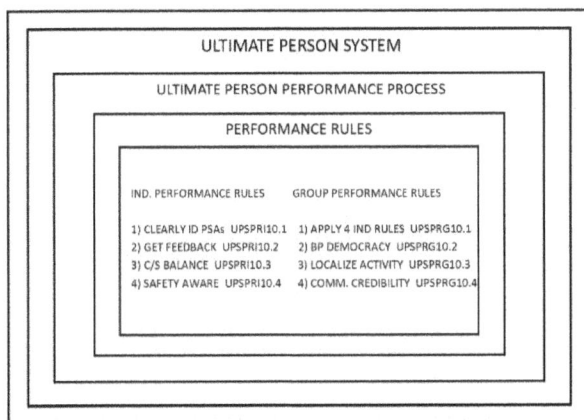

ULTIMATE PERSON SYSTEM

ULTIMATE PERSON PERFORMANCE PROCESS

PERFORMANCE RULES

IND. PERFORMANCE RULES   GROUP PERFORMANCE RULES

1) CLEARLY ID PSAs UPSPRI10.1   1) APPLY 4 IND RULES UPSPRG10.1
2) GET FEEDBACK UPSPRI10.2   2) BP DEMOCRACY UPSPRG10.2
3) C/S BALANCE UPSPRI10.3   3) LOCALIZE ACTIVITY UPSPRG10.3
4) SAFETY AWARE UPSPRI10.4   4) COMM. CREDIBILITY UPSPRG10.4

UW LEVEL 10 DIAGRAM

*The UW Level 10 diagram illustrates the identities of the individual
performance rules and the group performance rules. The individual
performance rules hypotheses are: 1) clearly identify PSAs Hypothesis
ID# = HUPSPRI10.1; 2) get feedback on progress Hypothesis ID# =
HUPSPRI10.2; 3) maintain challenge/skill balance Hypothesis ID# =
HUPSPRI10.3; and 4) maintain safety awareness Hypothesis ID# =
HUPSPRI10.4. The group performance rules hypotheses are: 1) apply
the four individual performance rules to groups Hypothesis ID# =
HUPSPRG10.1; 2) utilize a best practices democracy Hypothesis ID#
= HUPSPRG10.2; 3) localize your activity Hypothesis ID# = HUP-
SPRG10.3; and 4) communicate with credibility Hypothesis ID# =
HUPSPRG10.4.*

5

SUMMARY OF THE ULTIMATE WORLD PREDICTIONS

Predictions in science are logical deductions from hypotheses. The logical deductions are typically generalizations that a certain hypothesis – assuming the hypothesis holds true on a small scale – will also hold true on a larger scale.

UW Predictions are logical deductions from the UW Hypotheses. Remember that UW Hypotheses are explanations of why a certain PSA is necessary for human survival. The basic logical deduction from the hypotheses is that certain PSAs can be predicted to be performed on a larger scale, namely the scale of time, because they are necessary for human survival. Safety issues always have and always will take priority in human affairs, and human survival is the ultimate safety issue.

If these "do or die" PSAs are not performed in the future then there will be no future. So the future depends on these PSAs. Future proof yourself by learning all 70 of the UW predictions, and thereby learn a great deal about the world of the future.

But first, here are some of the key predictions given in this initial edition of UW theory, along with their associated hypotheses. These key predictions are:

* the person of the future
* the world of the future
* the technology of the future
* the economy of the future
* the communication format of the future.

In these key predictions given below, notice how the predictions are derived from the hypotheses. The predictions also share the same ID numbers as their associated hypothesis. The only difference is that the first digit in the predictions is a "P" for prediction instead of an "H" for hypothesis.

The Person of the Future

The person of the future, in terms of the skill set required for the future, is the Ultimate Person (UP). The definition of the UP is given is Characterization ID# = [C1.0]. The UP is defined as *a person who maximizes problem solving skill over time.* The specific hypothesis demonstrating the necessity of the UP is Hypothesis 1.0. Hypothesis 1.0 is also known as The Supreme Hypothesis, because it is the supreme solution to the human survival problem.

Here is Hypothesis ID# = [H1.0]

H1.0 Establishing and maintaining UP$_{MAX}$ is a necessary action because of the maximum problem complexity of the problem of surviving the universe using minimum resources, which requires maximum problem solving skill over time to resolve this maximum problem complexity.

Here is Prediction ID# = [P1.0]

P1.0 UP$_{MAX}$ will be established and maintained because it is necessary for human survival.

The World of the Future

The world of the future is the Ultimate World (UW). The definition of the UW is given in Characterization ID# = [C3.2]. The UW is defined as *a world-wide group of UPs that work together as a team to maximize group problem solving skill over time*. The specific hypothesis demonstrating the necessity of the UW is Hypothesis H3.2.

Here is Hypothesis ID# = [H3.2]

H3.2 Establishing and maintaining the Ultimate World is a necessary action because a world-wide group of UPs that work together as a team, is necessary to maximize group problem solving skill over time.

Here is Prediction ID# = [P3.2]

P3.2 The Ultimate World will be established and maintained because it is necessary for human survival.

The Technology of the Future

The technology of the future, in terms of information technology such as the internet and individual computing devices such as personal computers and cell phones, is the Human Survival Problem Solver (HSPS). The definition of the HSPS is given in Characterization ID# = [C3.1]. The HSPS is defined as *a world-wide, computer-based, solutions manager for managing all human survival problems in all safe locations of the universe and all time.* The specific hypothesis demonstrating the necessity of the HSPS is Hypothesis H3.1.

Here is Hypothesis ID# = [H3.1]

H3.1 Establishing and maintaining the Human Survival Problem Solver is a necessary action because a world-wide, computer-based, solutions manager is necessary to manage all human survival problems in all safe locations in the universe, and all time.

Here is Prediction ID# = [P3.1]

P3.1 The Human Survival Problem Solver will be established and maintained because it is necessary for human survival.

The Economy of the Future

The economy of the future is the Space Life Economy. The definition of The Space Life Economy is given in Characterization ID# = [CHAS6.3]. The Space Life Economy is defined *as a space-based economy similar to the current earth-based economy.* It is helpful to think of the current earth-based economy as a space-based economy that is in earth mode. The specific hypothesis demonstrating the necessity of the Space Life Economy is Hypothesis HHAS6.3.

Here is Hypothesis ID# = [HHAS6.3]

> HHAS6.3 Establishing and maintaining a Space Life Economy application is a necessary action because a space-based economy is necessary to maximize problem solving skill over time on the problem of managing a space-based economy.

Here is Prediction ID# = [PHAS6.3]

> PHAS6.2 A Space Life Economy application will be established and maintained because it is necessary for human survival.

The Communication Format of the Future

The future of communication, in terms of the format of communication, is UW Experiments. UW Experiments are defined as a scientific experiment that tests the necessity of a PSA. UW Experiments are the means by which PSAs are clearly identified, and clearly identifying PSAs will be the focus of all formal communication in the future. In essence, all formal communication in the future will focus on identifying the "do or die" actions for the world. It's a matter of survival.

The relevant characterization for UW Experiments is Characterization ID# = [CUPSPRI10.1]. The specific hypothesis demonstrating the necessity of UW Experiments is Hypothesis HUPSPRI10.1.

Here is Hypothesis ID# = [HUPSPRI10.1]

HUPSPRI10.1 Establishing and maintaining the performance rule of Clearly Identify PSAs is a necessary action because clearly identified PSAs are a condition of achieving Flow during PSA performance.

Here is Prediction ID# = [PUPSPRI10.1]

PUPSPRI10.1 Clearly Identify PSAs will be established and maintained as an individual performance rule because it is necessary for human survival.

The Complete List of UW Predictions

Here is the complete list of the UW Predictions, along with their associated diagrams. Please refer to the summary of the UW hypotheses given in the chapter 4 for the hypotheses associated with each prediction. Remember that the hypotheses and predictions are associated by their ID#.

There are a total of 70 predictions. The three predictions of the UW context are given first, following by the remaining 67 predictions which are listed from the top level down.

The Three Predictions from the UW Context

Prediction ID# = [PC1]
PC1 The human survival issue will be established and maintained as the most important issue because it is necessary for human survival.

Prediction ID# = [PC2]
PC2 A problem solving approach to the human survival issue based on maximum problem solving skill over time will be established and maintained because it is necessary for human survival.

Prediction ID# = [PC3]
PC3 A scientific solution to the human survival problem will be established and maintained because it is necessary for human survival.

The Top Level Prediction (The Supreme Prediction)

Prediction ID# = [P1.0]
P1.0 UP_{MAX} will be established and maintained because it is necessary for human survival.

Level 2 Predictions

Prediction ID# = [P2.1]
P2.1 UPs for all safe locations in the universe will be established and maintained because it is necessary for human survival.

Prediction ID# = [P2.2]
P2.2 Maximum group UP problem solving performance will be established and maintained because it is necessary for human survival.

Prediction ID# = [P2.3]
P2.3 UPs for all time will be established and maintained because it is necessary for human survival.

Level 3 Predictions

Prediction ID# = [P3.1]
P3.1 The Human Survival Problem Solver will be established and maintained because it is necessary for human survival.

Prediction ID# = [P3.2]
P3.2 The Ultimate World will be established and maintained because it is necessary for human survival.

Prediction ID# = [P3.3]
P3.3 A Control Theory Framework for integrating HSPS and
UW will be established and maintained because it is neces-
sary for human survival.

CONTROL THEORY FRAMEWORK

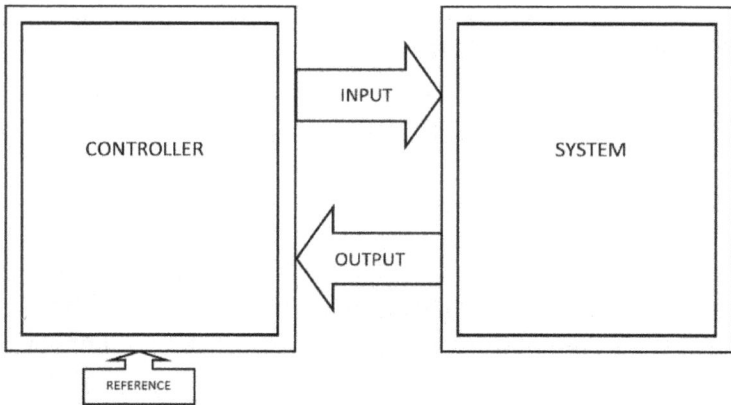

*The Control Theory Framework diagram (Prediction 3.3) illustrates
the framework of the five elements of a control system: the reference,
the controller, the input, the output and the system.*

ULTIMATE WORLD THEORY

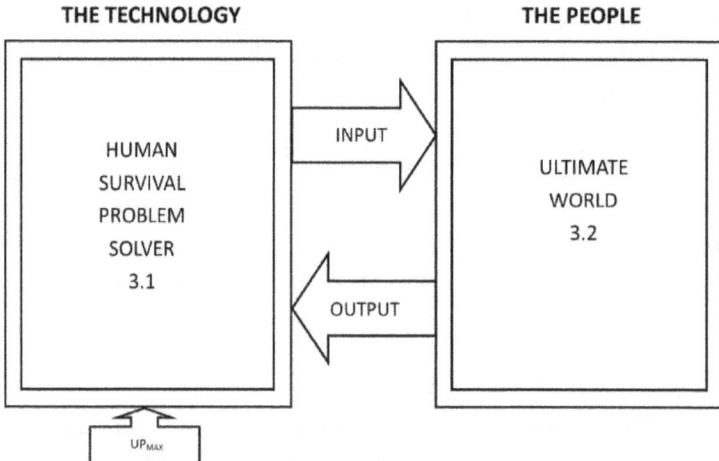

LEVEL 3 DIAGRAM

The Level 3 diagram illustrates how the Ultimate World (UW) and the Human Survival Problem Solver (HSPS) are integrated within the control theory framework. The UW (Prediction 3.2) is the system and HSPS (Prediction 3.1) is the controller.

IMPORTANT NOTE: Starting with Level 4, the UW Predictions (i.e. the people issues) are separated from the HSPS Predictions (i.e. the technology issues). The people issues are separated so that they can be given special attention. The Level 4 UW Predictions will start on page 154, and the Level 4 HSPS Predictions will continue here.

The HSPS Level 4 Predictions

HSPS Predictions

Prediction ID# = [PHC4.1]
PHC4.1 A controller within HSPS will be established and maintained because it is necessary for human survival.

Prediction ID# = [PHR4.1]
PHR4.1 A reference within HSPS will be established and maintained because it is necessary for human survival.

THE TECHNOLOGY

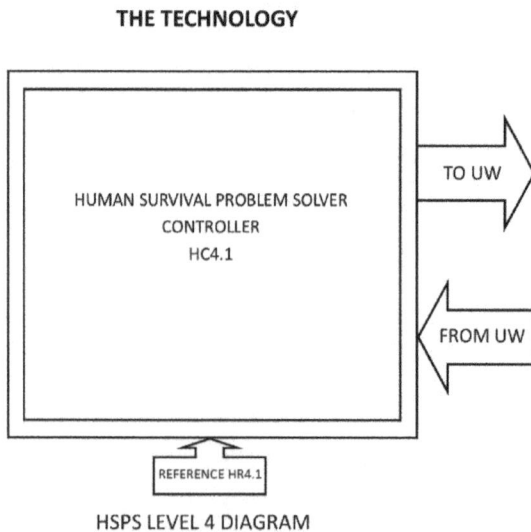

HUMAN SURVIVAL PROBLEM SOLVER
CONTROLLER
HC4.1

TO UW

FROM UW

REFERENCE HR4.1

HSPS LEVEL 4 DIAGRAM

The HSPS Level 4 diagram illustrates the two primary elements of the HSPS: the controller and the reference. Note that all HSPS elements have an "H" prefix on their identification numbers. Also note that the additional "P" prefix stands for "Prediction." For example, the HSPS controller prediction has the following identification number "PHC4.1."

The HSPS Level 5 Predictions

Controller Predictions

Prediction ID# = [PHC5.1]
PHC5.1 A HSPS expert system will be established and maintained because it is necessary for human survival.

Prediction ID# = [PHC5.2]
PHC5.2 A HSPS application set will be established and maintained because it is necessary for human survival.

Reference Prediction

Prediction ID# = [PHR5.1]
PHR5.1 UP_{MAX} will be established and maintained as the HSPS reference because it is necessary for human survival.

THE TECHNOLOGY

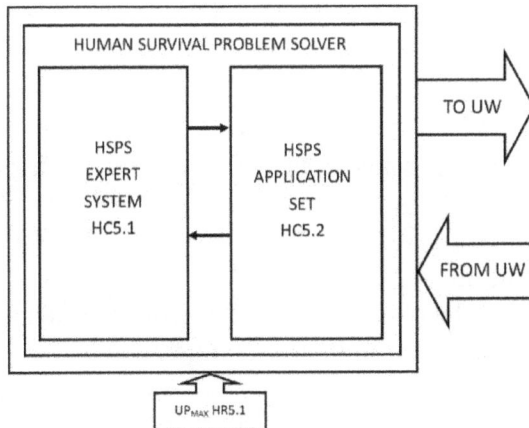

HSPS LEVEL 5 DIAGRAM

The HSPS Level 5 diagram illustrates the two primary elements of the HSPS controller: the HSPS expert system prediction is Prediction ID# = PHC5.1; and the HSPS application set prediction is Prediction ID#

= PHC5.2. Plus the HSPS reference of UP$_{MAX}$prediction is Prediction ID# = PHR5.1.

The HSPS Level 6 Predictions

HSPS Expert System Predictions

Prediction ID# = [PHES6.1]
PHES6.1 A HSPS knowledge base will be established and maintained because it is necessary for human survival.

Prediction ID# = [PHES6.2]
PHES6.2 A HSPS inference engine will be established and maintained because it is necessary for human survival.

Prediction ID# = [PHES6.3]
PHES6.3 A HSPS user interface will be established and maintained because it is necessary for human survival.

HSPS Application Set Predictions

Prediction ID# = [PHAS6.1]
PHAS6.1 A UW Theory Education application will be established and maintained because it is necessary for human survival.

Prediction ID# = [PHAS6.2]
PHAS6.2 A Human Survival Problem Identification application will be established and maintained because it is necessary for human survival.

Prediction ID# = [PHAS6.3]
PHAS6.3 A Space Life Economy application will be established and maintained because it is necessary for human survival.

Prediction ID# = [PHAS6.4]
PHAS6.4 A Safety Awareness application will be established
and maintained because it is necessary for human survival.

THE TECHNOLOGY

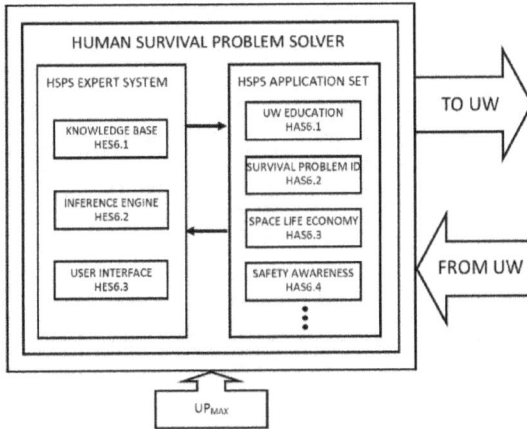

HSPS LEVEL 6 DIAGRAM

*The HSPS Level 6 diagram illustrates the detailed elements within the
HSPS expert system and the HSPS application set. The knowledge base
prediction is Prediction ID# = PHES6.1. The inference engine prediction is Prediction ID# = PHES6.2. The user interface prediction is
Prediction ID# = PHES6.3. The UW education application prediction
is Prediction ID# = PHAS6.1. The human survival problem application
prediction is Prediction ID# = PHAS6.2. The space life economy application prediction is Prediction ID# = PHAS6.3. The safety awareness application prediction is Prediction ID# = PHAS6.4.*

The HSPS Level 7 Predictions

Knowledge Base Predictions

Prediction ID# = [PHKB7.1]

PHKB7.1 A definition knowledge base will be established and maintained because it is necessary for human survival.

Prediction ID# = [PHKB7.2]
PHKB7.2 A performance knowledge base will be established and maintained because it is necessary for human survival

THE TECHNOLOGY

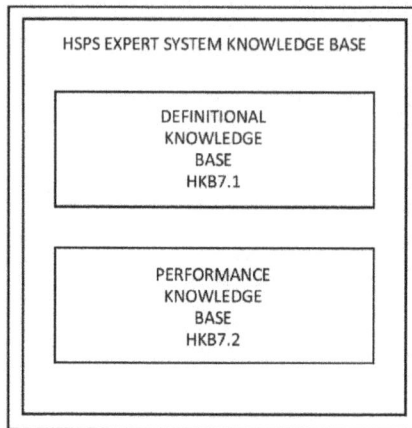

HSPS EXPERT SYSTEM KNOWLEDGE BASE

DEFINITIONAL
KNOWLEDGE
BASE
HKB7.1

PERFORMANCE
KNOWLEDGE
BASE
HKB7.2

HSPS LEVEL 7 DIAGRAM 1

The HSPS Level 7 diagram 1 illustrates the two knowledge bases within the HSPS expert system knowledge base. The definitional knowledge base prediction is Prediction ID# = PHKB7.1. The performance knowledge base prediction is Prediction ID# = PHKB7.2.

Inference Engine Predictions

Prediction ID# = [PHIE7.1]
PHIE7.1 A definitional inference rule will be established and maintained because it is necessary for human survival.
Prediction ID# = [PHIE7.2]

PHIE7.2 A performance inference rule will be established and maintained because it is necessary for human survival.

THE TECHNOLOGY

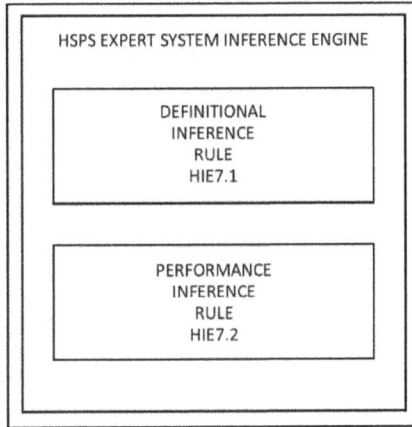

```
┌─────────────────────────────────────────┐
│ HSPS EXPERT SYSTEM INFERENCE ENGINE       │
│   ┌───────────────────────────────┐       │
│   │      DEFINITIONAL              │       │
│   │      INFERENCE                 │       │
│   │      RULE                      │       │
│   │      HIE7.1                    │       │
│   └───────────────────────────────┘       │
│   ┌───────────────────────────────┐       │
│   │      PERFORMANCE               │       │
│   │      INFERENCE                 │       │
│   │      RULE                      │       │
│   │      HIE7.2                    │       │
│   └───────────────────────────────┘       │
└─────────────────────────────────────────┘
```

HSPS LEVEL 7 DIAGRAM 2

The HSPS Level 7 diagram 2 illustrates the two elements of the HSPS expert system inference engine. The definitional inference rule prediction is Prediction ID# = PHIE7.1. The performance inference rule prediction is Prediction ID# = PHIE7.2

User Interface Predictions

Prediction ID# = [PHUI7.1]
PHUI7.1 A user input/output section of the user interface will be established and maintained because it is necessary for human survival.

Prediction ID# = [PHUI7.2]
PHUI7.2 A PSA list section of the user interface will be established and maintained because it is necessary for human survival.

Prediction ID# = [PHUI7.3]
PHUI7.3 A support section of the user interface will be established and maintained because it is necessary for human survival.

THE TECHNOLOGY

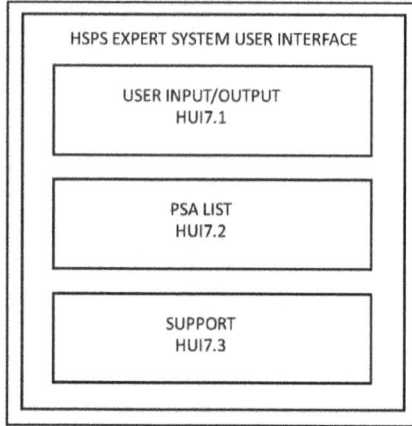

```
┌─────────────────────────────────┐
│ ┌─────────────────────────────┐ │
│ │ HSPS EXPERT SYSTEM USER INTERFACE │
│ │  ┌───────────────────────┐  │ │
│ │  │   USER INPUT/OUTPUT   │  │ │
│ │  │       HUI7.1          │  │ │
│ │  └───────────────────────┘  │ │
│ │  ┌───────────────────────┐  │ │
│ │  │      PSA LIST         │  │ │
│ │  │       HUI7.2          │  │ │
│ │  └───────────────────────┘  │ │
│ │  ┌───────────────────────┐  │ │
│ │  │      SUPPORT          │  │ │
│ │  │       HUI7.3          │  │ │
│ │  └───────────────────────┘  │ │
│ └─────────────────────────────┘ │
└─────────────────────────────────┘
```

HSPS LEVEL 7 DIAGRAM 3

The HSPS Level 7 diagram 3 illustrates the three elements of the HSPS expert system user interface. The user input/output prediction is Prediction ID# = PHUI7.1. The PSA list prediction is Prediction ID# = PHUI7.2. The support prediction is Prediction ID# = PHUI7.3.

UW Theory Education Application Predictions

UW Theory Online Course Prediction

Prediction ID# = [PHASU7.1]
PHASU7.1 A UW Theory online course will be established and maintained because it is necessary for human survival.
UP Skill Online Course Prediction

Prediction ID# = [PHASU7.2]
PHASU7.2 A UP Skill online course will be established and maintained because it is necessary for human survival.

THE TECHNOLOGY

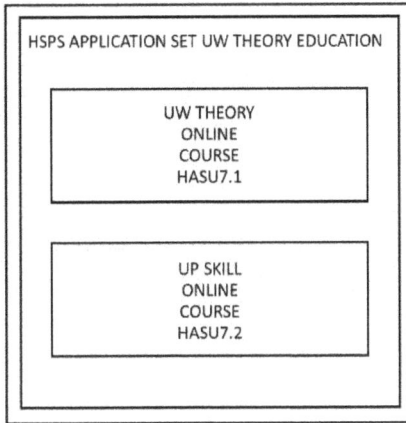

```
┌─────────────────────────────────────────┐
│ ┌───────────────────────────────────────┐ │
│ │ HSPS APPLICATION SET UW THEORY EDUCATION │ │
│ │                                         │ │
│ │   ┌─────────────────────────────┐       │ │
│ │   │        UW THEORY            │       │ │
│ │   │        ONLINE              │       │ │
│ │   │        COURSE              │       │ │
│ │   │        HASU7.1             │       │ │
│ │   └─────────────────────────────┘       │ │
│ │                                         │ │
│ │   ┌─────────────────────────────┐       │ │
│ │   │        UP SKILL            │       │ │
│ │   │        ONLINE              │       │ │
│ │   │        COURSE              │       │ │
│ │   │        HASU7.2             │       │ │
│ │   └─────────────────────────────┘       │ │
│ │                                         │ │
│ └───────────────────────────────────────┘ │
└─────────────────────────────────────────┘
```

HSPS LEVEL 7 DIAGRAM 4

The HSPS Level 7 diagram 4 illustrates the two online courses within the UW Theory education application. The UW Theory online course prediction is Prediction ID# = PHAS7.1. The UW Skill online course prediction is Prediction ID# = PHAS7.2. Since these two courses are already available, these two predictions have actually held true!

IMPORTANT NOTE: The next section on the UW Predictions is separate from the HSPS Predictions. The UW Predictions start at Level 4.

The UW Level 4 Predictions

Prediction ID# = [PUR4.1]
PUR4.1 A reference for the UW will be established and maintained because it is necessary for human survival.

Prediction ID# = [PUC4.1]
PUC4.1 A controller for the UW will be established and maintained because it is necessary for human survival.

Prediction ID# = [PUI4.1]
PUI4.1 An input to the UW will be established and maintained because it is necessary for human survival.

Prediction ID# = [PUO4.1]
PUO4.1 An output from the UW will be established and maintained because it is necessary for human survival.

Prediction ID# = [PUS4.1]
PUS4.1 A system within the UW will be established and maintained because it is necessary for human survival.

THE PEOPLE

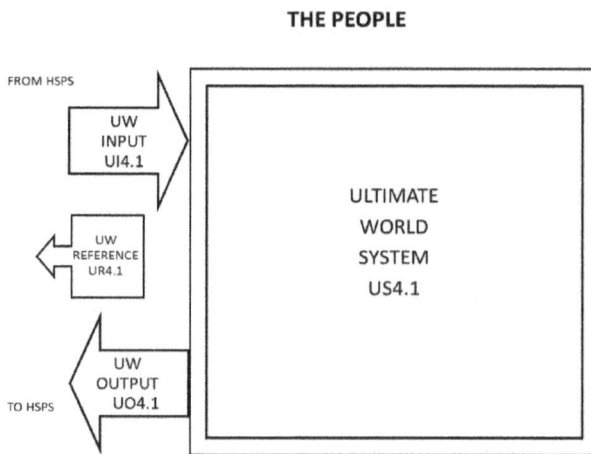

UW LEVEL 4 DIAGRAM

The UW Level 4 diagram illustrates the five elements of the UW control system. The UW reference prediction is Prediction ID# = PUR4.1. The UW input prediction is Prediction ID# = PUI4.1. The UW output prediction is Prediction ID# = PUO4.1. The UW system prediction is Prediction ID# = PUS4.1. Note that the UW controller is the HSPS which is detailed earlier in this chapter.

The UW Level 5 Predictions

UW Reference Predictions

Prediction ID# = [PUR5.1]
PUR5.1 UP$_{MAX}$ will be established and maintained as the UW reference because it is necessary for survival.

UW Controller Predictions

Prediction ID# = [PUC5.1]
PUC5.1 The HSPS will be established and maintained as the UW controller because it is necessary for human survival.

UW Input Predictions

Prediction ID# = [PUI5.1]
PUI5.1 New PSAs will be established and maintained as a UW input because it is necessary for human survival.

Prediction ID# = [PUI5.2]
PUI5.2 Paychecks will be established and maintained as a UW input because it is necessary for human survival.

Prediction ID# = [PUI5.3]
PUI5.3 New non-UPs will be established and maintained as a UW input because it is necessary for human survival.

UW Output Predictions

Prediction ID# = [PUO5.1]
PUO5.1 Performance results will be established and maintained as a UW output because it is necessary for human survival.

Prediction ID# = [PUO5.2]
PUO5.2 UP_N will be established and maintained as a UW output because it is necessary for human survival.

UW System Prediction

Prediction ID# = [PUS5.1]
PUS5.1 Uniquely identified UPs from UP1 to UP_N will be established and maintained as the UW system because it is necessary for human survival.

THE PEOPLE

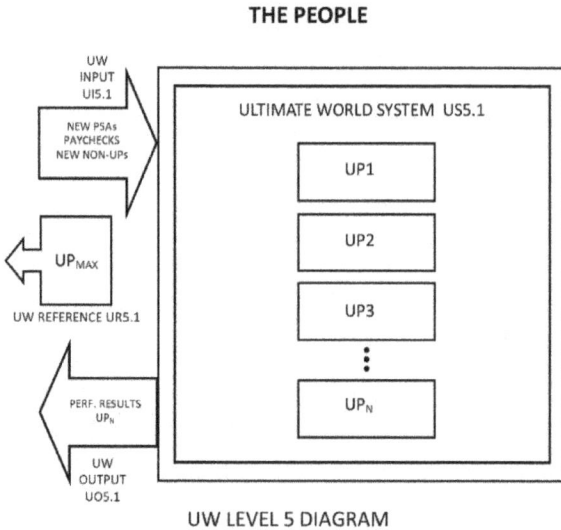

UW LEVEL 5 DIAGRAM

The UW Level 5 diagram identifies the predictions of the five elements of the UW control system. The UW reference (UP_{MAX}) prediction is

Prediction ID# = PUR5.1. The UW input predictions (new PSAs, paychecks, new non-UPs) are Prediction ID# = PUI5.1-PUI5.3. The UW output predictions (performance results, UP$_N$) are Prediction ID# = PUO5.1-PUO5.2. The UW system prediction (UP1- UP$_N$) is Prediction ID# = PUS5.1. Note that the UW controller is the HSPS which is detailed in chapter 2.

The UW Level 6 Predictions

UP Predictions

Prediction ID# = [PUPR6.1]
PUPR6.1 A reference for each UP will be established and maintained because it is necessary for human survival.

Prediction ID# = [PUPC6.2]
PUPC6.2 A controller for each UP will be established and maintained because it is necessary for human survival.

Prediction ID# = [PUPI6.3]
PUPI6.3 An input for each UP will be established and maintained because it is necessary for human survival.

Prediction ID# = [PUPO6.4]
PUPO6.4 An output for each UP will be established and maintained because it is necessary for human survival.

Prediction ID# = [PUPS6.5]
PUPS6.5 A system for each UP will be established and maintained because it is necessary for human survival.

THE PEOPLE

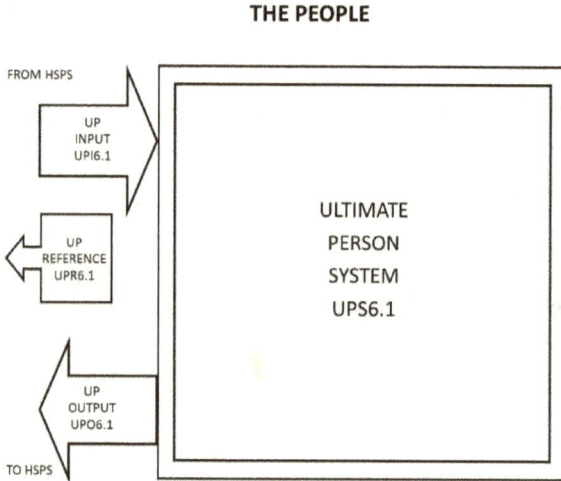

UW LEVEL 6 DIAGRAM

The UW Level 6 diagram illustrates the five elements of the UP control system. The UP reference prediction is Prediction ID# = PUPR6.1. The UP input prediction is Prediction ID# = PUPI6.1. The UP output prediction is Prediction ID# = PUPO6.1. The UP system prediction is Prediction ID# = PUPS6.1. Note that the UP controller is the HSPS, which is detailed in chapter 2.

The UW Level 7 Predictions

UP Reference Prediction

Prediction ID# = [PPPR7.1]
PPPR7.1 Maximum personal problem solving skill, and maximum professional problem solving skill will be established and maintained as the UP reference because it is necessary for human survival.

UP Controller Prediction

Prediction ID# = [PPPC7.1]
PPPC7.1 The HSPS will be established and maintained as the UP controller for each UP because it is necessary for human survival.

UP Input Predictions

Prediction ID# = [PPPI7.1]
PPPI7.1 New PSAs will be established and maintained as an input to each UP because it is necessary for human survival.

Prediction ID# = [PPPI7.2]
PPPI7.2 Paychecks will be established and maintained as an input to each UP because it is necessary for human survival.

UP Output Prediction

Prediction ID# = [PPPO7.1]
PPPO7.1 Performance results will be established and maintained as the UP output because it is necessary for human survival.

UP System Prediction

Prediction ID# = [PPPS7.1]
PPPS7.1 The Ultimate Person Performance Process (UPPP) will be established and maintained as the UP system because it is necessary for human survival.

THE PEOPLE

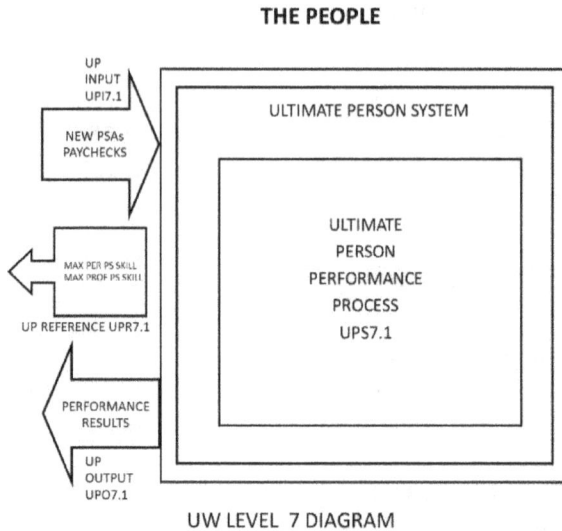

UW LEVEL 7 DIAGRAM

The UW Level 7 diagram illustrates the identities of each of the five elements of the UP control system. The UP reference prediction (max personal problem solving skill and maximum professional problem solving skill) is Prediction ID# = PUPR7.1. The UP input prediction (new PSAs, paychecks) is Prediction ID# = PUPI7.1. The UP output (performance results) prediction is Prediction ID# = PUPO7.1. The UP system (UPPP) prediction is Prediction ID# = PUPS7.1. And re-member the UP controller is the HSPS, which is detailed earlier in this chapter.

The UW Level 8 Predictions

UPPP Predictions

Prediction ID# = [PUPSU8.1]
PUPSU8.1 Establishing and maintaining Define Problem as Step 1 of the UPPP is a necessary action because Define Problem is a necessary first step of maximizing performance and happiness.

Prediction ID# = [PUPSU8.2]
PUPSU8.2 Establishing and maintaining Define Solution (PSAs) as Step 2 of the UPPP is a necessary action because Define Solution (PSAs) is a necessary second step of maximizing performance and happiness.

Prediction ID# = [PUPSU8.3]
PUPSU8.3 Establishing and maintaining Perform Solution (PSAs) as Step 3 of the UPPP is a necessary action because Perform Solution (PSAs) is a necessary third step of maximizing performance and happiness.

Prediction ID# = [PUPSU8.4]
PUPSU8.4 Establishing and maintaining Evaluate Results as Step 4 of the UPPP is a necessary action because Evaluate Results is a necessary fourth step of maximizing performance and happiness.

Prediction ID# = [PUPSU8.5]
PUPSU8.5 Establishing and maintaining Repeat Steps 2-4 continuously on new solutions as Step 5 of the UPPP is a necessary action because Repeat Steps 2-4 continuously on new solutions is a necessary fifth step of maximizing performance and happiness.

Prediction ID# = [PUPSU8.6]
PUPSU8.6 Establishing and maintaining Perfect the UPPP and Have Fun as Step 4 of the UPPP is a necessary action because Perfect the UPPP and Have Fun is a necessary sixth step of maximizing performance and happiness.

Prediction ID# = [PUPSPR8.1]
PUPSPR8.1 Performance rules will be established for UPPP because they are necessary for human survival.

THE PEOPLE

```
┌─────────────────────────────────────────────────┐
│ ┌─────────────────────────────────────────────┐ │
│ │           ULTIMATE PERSON SYSTEM              │ │
│ │  ┌───────────────────────────────────────┐   │ │
│ │  │  ULTIMATE PERSON PERFORMANCE PROCESS   │   │ │
│ │  │                                        │   │ │
│ │  │  STEP 1 DEFINE PROBLEM      UPSU8.1    │   │ │
│ │  │  STEP 2 DEFINE SOLUTION     UPSU8.2    │   │ │
│ │  │  STEP 3 PERFORM SOLUTION    UPSU8.3    │   │ │
│ │  │  STEP 4 EVALUATE RESULTS    UPSU8.4    │   │ │
│ │  │  STEP 5 REPEAT STEPS 2-4    UPSU8.5    │   │ │
│ │  │  STEP 6 PERFECT UPPP        UPSU8.6    │   │ │
│ │  │                                        │   │ │
│ │  │  PERFORMANCE RULES          UPSPR8.1   │   │ │
│ │  └───────────────────────────────────────┘   │ │
│ └─────────────────────────────────────────────┘ │
└─────────────────────────────────────────────────┘
```

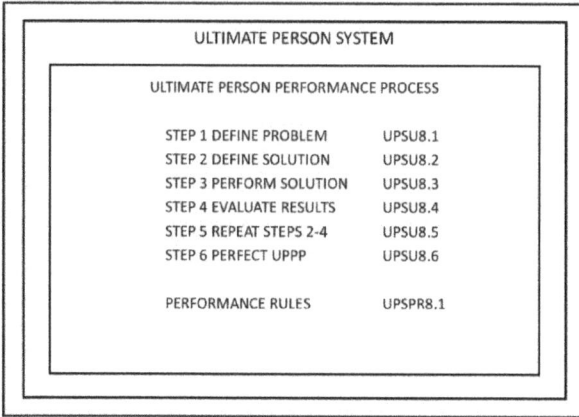

UW LEVEL 8 DIAGRAM

The UW Level 8 diagram illustrates the six steps of the UPPP and the performance rules. The UPPP Step 1 prediction (Define Problem) is Prediction ID# = PPPSM8.1. The UPPP Step 2 prediction (Define Solution) is Prediction ID# = PPPSM8.2. The UPPP Step 3 prediction (Perform Solution) is Prediction ID# = PPPSM8.3. The UPPP Step 4 prediction (Evaluate results) is Prediction ID# = PUPSU8.4. The UPPP Step 5 prediction (Repeat Steps 2-4 continuously) is Prediction ID# = PUPSU8.5. The UPPP Step 6 prediction (Perfect UPPP) is Prediction ID# = PUPSU8.6. And the Performance Rules prediction is Prediction ID# = PUPSPR8.1.

The UW Level 9 Predictions

Performance Rules Prediction

Prediction ID# = [PUPSPR9.1]
PUPSPR9.1 Individual performance rules will be established and maintained because they are necessary for human survival.

Prediction ID# = [PUPSPR9.2]
PUPSPR9.2 Group performance rules will be established and maintained because they are necessary for human survival.

THE PEOPLE

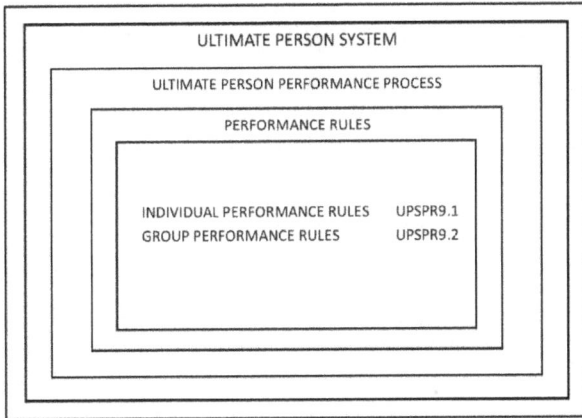

UW LEVEL 9 DIAGRAM

The UW Level 9 diagram illustrates the two types of performance rules: individual and group. The individual performance rules prediction is Prediction ID# = PUPSPR9.1. The group performance rules prediction is Prediction ID# = PUPSPR9.2.

The UW Level 10 Predictions

Individual Performance Rules Predictions

Prediction ID# = [PUPSPRI10.1]
PUPSPRI10.1 Clearly Identify PSAs will be established and maintained as an individual performance rule because it is necessary for human survival.

Prediction ID# = [PUPSPRI10.2]
PUPSPRI10.2 Get Feedback on Progress will be established
and maintained as an individual performance rule because it
is necessary for human survival.

Prediction ID# = [PUPSPRI10.3]
PUPSPR10.3 Maintain Challenge/Skill Balance will be established and maintained as an individual performance rule
because it is necessary for human survival.

Prediction ID# = [PUPSPRI10.4]
PUPSPRI10.4 Maintain Safety Awareness will be established and maintained as an individual performance rule because it is necessary for human survival.

Group Performance Rules Predictions

Prediction ID# = [PUPSPRG10.1]
PUPSPRG10.1 Apply Individual Performance Rules to the
Group will be established and maintained as a group perfor-
mance rule because it is necessary for human survival.

Prediction ID# = [PUPSPRG10.2]
PUPSPRG10.2 Utilize a Best Practices Democracy will be
established and maintained as a group performance rule because it is necessary for human survival.

Prediction ID# = [PUPSPRG10.3]
PUPSPRG10.3 Localize Your Activity will be established
and maintained as a group performance rule because it is necessary for human survival.

Prediction ID# = [PUPSPRG10.4]
PUPSPRG10.4 Communicate With Credibility will be established and maintained as a group performance rule because it
is necessary for human survival.

THE PEOPLE

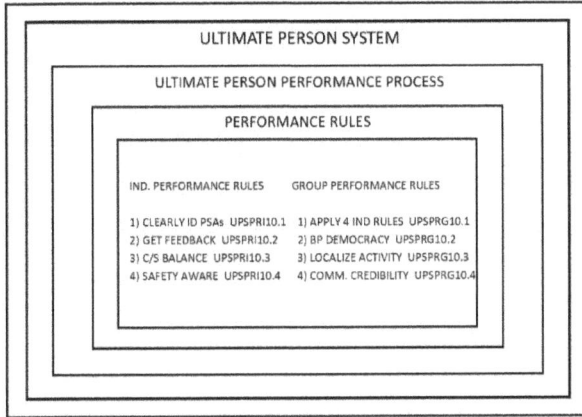

ULTIMATE PERSON SYSTEM

ULTIMATE PERSON PERFORMANCE PROCESS

PERFORMANCE RULES

IND. PERFORMANCE RULES	GROUP PERFORMANCE RULES
1) CLEARLY ID PSAs UPSPRI10.1	1) APPLY 4 IND RULES UPSPRG10.1
2) GET FEEDBACK UPSPRI10.2	2) BP DEMOCRACY UPSPRG10.2
3) C/S BALANCE UPSPRI10.3	3) LOCALIZE ACTIVITY UPSPRG10.3
4) SAFETY AWARE UPSPRI10.4	4) COMM. CREDIBILITY UPSPRG10.4

UW LEVEL 10 DIAGRAM

The UW Level 10 diagram illustrates the identities of the individual performance rules and the group performance rules.

The predictions of the individual performance rules are: 1) clearly identify PSAs Prediction ID# = PUPSPRI10.1; 2) get feedback on progress Prediction ID# = PUPSPRI10.2; 3) maintain challenge/skill balance Prediction ID# = PUPSPRI10.3; 4) maintain safety awareness Prediction ID# = PUPSPRI10.4.

The predictions of the group performance rules are: 1) apply the four individual performance rules to the group Prediction ID# = PUPSPRG10.1; 2) utilize a best practices democracy Prediction ID# = PUPSPRG10.2; 3) localize your activity Prediction ID# = PUPSPRG10.3; 4) communicate with credibility Prediction ID# = PUPSPRG10.

6

ULTIMATE WORLD
EXPERIMENTS

A simplified version of communication in the future is people saying one of two things to each other: 1) "we need to do this because it is necessary for human survival of the universe"; or 2) "we don't need to do this because it is not necessary for human survival of the universe." A scientific version of communication in the future is people performing UW experiments.

Communication by means of UW experiments is the future of communication because UW experiments are the means to scientifically define and verify PSA necessity (i.e. the actions that are "do or die" for the world). Without UW experiments, we will not know the actions that are "do or die", and therefore, will not know to perform them. If the "do or die" actions are not performed, then the human species will become extinct, and there will be no future. *Simply put, the future depends on UW experiments.*

Prediction PUPSPRI10.1 is the formal statement of why UW experiments are the future of communication:

> Prediction ID# [PUPSPRI10.1]
>
> PUPSPRI10.1 Clearly Identify PSAs will be established and maintained as an individual performance rule because it is necessary for human survival.

Remember that UW Experiments are the means by which all PSAs are clearly identified.

The UW Experiment Form

The key to a good UW experiment (and therefore good communication) is credibility in your experiment. Credible communication is defined here as having two primary elements:

> 1) direct relevance to the super-problem of human survival; and
> 2) correct science - this involves carefully using the scientific method to ensure accuracy, reliability, objectivity, and testability in the terminology.

The UW Experiment Form facilitates credible communication by ensuring the inclusion of both of these elements. The hierarchical problem structure built into the PSA characterizations ensures relevance to the super-problem of human survival. And the Reason for Necessity data field provides the logical coherence that holds the hierarchical problem structure together.

ULTIMATE WORLD THEORY
EXPERIMENT FORM

UW CHARACTERIZATIONS

Characterization ID#: _____
Problem Solving Action (PSA) ID#:_____
PSA Name: _____
Problem ID#: _____
Problem Name: _____
Action Name: _____
Reason For Necessity: _____
Unit of Analysis: _____
Time Deadline: _____
Success Measure: _____
Supplemental Definitions: _____
Supplemental Reasoning: _____

UW HYPOTHESIS

Hypothesis ID# _____
[PSA name]: _____
is a necessary action because [Reason for Necessity]: _____

_____

UW PREDICTION

Prediction ID# _____
[Problem Name] _____
will be [Action Name] _____
because it is necessary for human survival.

UW EXPERIMENT

Experiment ID# _____
Experiment Type: ADD   DELETE

ADD PSA
[PSA name]: _____
is a necessary action because [Reason for Necessity]: _____

_____

DELETE PSA
[PSA name]: _____
is not a necessary action because [Reason for Not-Necessity]: _____

_____

The UW Experiment Form also facilitates correct science by identifying the necessary data for all four of the four steps of the UW scientific method (which is derived directly from the basic scientific method – see Appendix A1).

The UW Experiment Form will become the new standard form for credible communication. Performing a UW experiment – and therefore performing credible science – is a simple as filling out this one-page form.

Types of UW Experiments

The UW Experiment Form includes two additional data fields (in addition to the eleven standard PSA data fields). These additional data fields specify the Experiment ID#, and the Experiment Type (either ADD PSA or DELETE PSA).

ADD PSA experiments focus on adding a new PSA, and are justified by means of a Reason for Necessity. DELETE PSA experiments focus on deleting an existing PSA, and are justified by means of a Reason for Not-necessity. A Reason for Not-necessity is simply the converse of a Reason for Necessity. It is a reason why a certain PSA is not necessary.

The process of updating an existing PSA is a two-step process of first deleting a PSA, and then adding the new PSA with the new updated information.

Example UW Experiments

This book contains numerous examples of UW experiments. Each of the UW Hypotheses listed in Chapter 4 is actually an ADD PSA Experiment. So there are currently 70 UW experiments and counting. The future of communication is here!

Although this initial set of hypotheses is just a starting point for a fully detailed UW theory, it is a good starting point. The big issues of UW theory – namely, the context of UW, the science of UW, and the practice of UW – have been accurately and reliably defined. And the UW scientific method provides a scientific method for identifying the remaining details (i.e. the remaining PSAs).

Formal vs. Informal Communication

All formal communication in the future will be performed using the UW Experiment Form. It identifies all the necessary information for a credible UW experiment, and the correct format for this information.

Informal communication will be performed through informal statements that discuss the necessity of a PSA. The primary informal statements are "we need to do PSA ID# [ ] because of Reason for Necessity ID# [ ]", and "we don't need to do PSA ID# [ ] because of Reason for Necessity ID# [ ]." The primary benefit of informal communication is brainstorming on the necessity of PSAs. This brainstorming can preliminarily identify new PSAs that are necessary, and those that are not necessary. Once a preliminary experiment makes sense, it can be then be formalized through the UW experiment form.

Note that during informal communication, the more detailed a statement is, the more credible it is. Overall, we need to move away from the opinionated bickering (and the fake news) that is so prevalent in the world today. And we need to move toward formal UW experiments. This is not to say that we need to eliminate free speech. There will always be a need for free speech. However, we need to move in the direction of credible speech using the UW Experiment Form. It's a matter of human survival.

Manual vs. Semi-Automatic Communication

The UW Experiment Form provides for a manual mode of communication, both formal and informal. It also provides for the underlying knowledge bases of HSPS functionality.

When the HSPS is implemented, the HSPS will facilitate semi-automatic communication through the computer. Eventually, all formal communication will be done semi-automatically through the HSPS.

Keep in mind that the HSPS knowledge base will be supplied with human intelligence that will come from human experts. And it will established and maintained by humans with safety provisions built into it. For safety reasons, we can never have fully automatic communication through the computer.

CONCLUSION

This book marks the debut of Ultimate World Theory (UW Theory). It is a scientific theory of how the entire world can work together as a problem solving team to solve all the world's problems and have fun doing it.

The scientific *Theory* part of the title demonstrates the credibility of the way the subject is defined and communicated. Scientific communication is credible because it focuses on accuracy, reliability, objectivity, and testability.

The science is presented in a way that is well-grounded in established science, yet is also super-innovative. The primary way it is well-grounded is by being based on the basic scientific method that has been established for centuries. All the great scientific discoveries in medicine, physics, engineering, chemistry, biology, psychology, etc., were based on the same basic scientific method. The UW scientific method is derived directly from the same basic scientific method as all these other great scientific discoveries. UW Theory was developed by applying this established method to the human survival problem which is the ultimate problem.

UW Theory is also super-innovative and contains a long list of innovations. Two of the major innovations are: 1) a scientific method for identifying the actions that are necessary for human survival (namely, the UW Scientific Method); and 2) an action performance process for maximizing both performance results and happiness (namely, the Ultimate Person Performance Process). *By applying this action performance process to the actions that are necessary for human survival, the world can truly solve the human survival problem, and have fun doing it.*

A third major innovation is a new knowledge type called *necessitive* knowledge. The vast majority of science is *descriptive* and describes "the way things are." Necessitive knowledge is different and defines "the way things need to be." The word necessitive is a new term defined here for the first time. It makes for a convenient comparison to the conventional descriptive science.

Necessitive knowledge is knowledge of the actions necessary for human survival (i.e. the "do or die" actions), thereby making necessitive science *the science of do or die for the world.*

Necessitive knowledge is very powerful knowledge. For example, it can be used to accurately predict the future. The predictions come directly from the do or die actions. The reasoning is that if the do or die actions are not successfully performed, then there will be no future. So the future is dependent on the do or die actions being successfully performed.

Furthermore, safety issues always have and always will take priority in human affairs. Human survival problems are the ultimate safety issues, and as such, they will always take priority in world events. The Coronavirus pandemic is an excellent example of how a human survival problem takes priority in world events.

Some of the key predictions derived from UW Theory are:

a) the future of individual people – in terms of their skill set
b) the future of the world – in terms of how people will socialize and interact
c) the future of technology – in terms of the internet and individual computing devices such as personal computers and cell phones
d) the future economy – in terms of the businesses and jobs
e) the future of communication – in terms of the format of communication

All of these predictions are accurate, reliable, objective and testable because they are based on the established scientific method. Chapter 5 summarizes an initial set of 70 predictions. There will be many more.

The most important prediction of all is the future of the individual person. This prediction is made in terms of the skills that the person of the future will require. The person of the future is defined as an Ultimate Person (UP). The basic definition of the UP is *a person who maximizes problem solving skill over time.*

The solution to the human survival problem is simply to maximize the number of UPs. The leads us to The Supreme Hypothesis, which is a hypothesis of the solution to the human survival problem. Here is The Supreme Hypothesis:

Hypothesis ID# = [H1.0]
H1.0 Establishing and maintaining UP_{MAX} is a necessary action because of the maximum problem complexity of the human survival problem, which requires maximum problem solving skill over time to resolve this maximum problem complexity.

The short form of The Supreme Hypothesis is simply:

$$UW = UP_{MAX}$$

All the other hypotheses within UW Theory, each defining a do or die action, are derived directly from The Supreme Hypothesis. There are 70 hypotheses in this initial edition of UW Theory. There will be many more.

The Supreme Solution to the Human Survival Problem

There are five primary reasons why The Supreme Hypothesis of "Establishing and maintaining UP_{MAX}" is the supreme solution to the human survival problem:

1) UP_{MAX} leads to maximum clarity of problem identification – maximizing problem solving skill over time includes the skill of clearly identifying problems. The human survival problem is defined in terms of the threats to human survival. By applying maximum skill to the process of identifying the threats to human survival, we can obtain the most clear and accurate list of the threats.

2) UP_{MAX} leads to maximum problem solving performance – maximizing problem solving skill over time includes a process for performing the "do or die" actions in a way that maximizes performance results. This process is called the Ultimate Person Performance Process (UPPP). In the event of a threat to human survival, we need to take action to eliminate the threat, not just identify the threat. And not only does this process maximize performance results on the top level problem of human survival, but on all the world's problems.

3) UP_{MAX} leads to maximum individual and world happiness – maximizing problem solving skill over time also leads to maximum happiness. The science of happiness, which is built into UW Theory by means of the UPPP performance rules, shows us that maximum happiness and maximum performance are directly linked. This applies to both individual and group happiness.

4) UP$_{MAX}$ leads to maximum improvement over time – maximizing problem solving skill over time includes a built-in feedback mechanism which facilitates critical feedback on problem solving performance. This feedback is then used to correct mistakes, adapt to change, deal with unknowns, maintain stability, and improve performance results over time. This feedback mechanism is the control theory framework which is identified in Hypothesis 3.3. Most of the diagrams in this book are based on the control theory framework.

5) UP$_{MAX}$ can be stated with certainty. We can be certain about the need to maximize problem solving skill over time. This is due to maximum problem complexity of the human survival problem imposed by the universe.

This certainty about the need for UP$_{MAX}$ validates the Supreme Hypothesis as a correct hypothesis. UW Theory is therefore a credible theory, and is therefore the truth. Problem identification, problem solving performance, happiness, improvement over time and certainty are all validated. *The net result of UW theory is the truth about how the world can solve the human survival problem, and have fun doing it.*

The credibility of the Supreme Hypothesis is further demonstrated by its format which is designed for testability. Experiments on the Supreme Hypothesis (and any other hypothesis within UW Theory) are not only welcome, but encouraged. An entire chapter of this book (Chapter 6) is devoted to performing UW experiments, and communicating with credibility.

Mandatory Nature

UW Theory is mandatory learning for everyone in the world. The reasoning is as simple as 1-2-3.

1) First, UW Theory provides the knowledge that people need in order to maximize their problem solving skill over time.

2) Second, all people need to maximize their problem solving skill over time so that the world as a whole can maximize its problem solving skill over time.

3) Third, the world as a whole needs to maximize its problem solving skill over time to resolve the maximum problem complexity of the human survival problem imposed by the universe.

The bottom line is that UW Theory is mandatory learning for everyone because it is a matter of human survival and is therefore do or die for the world. And maximum problem solving skill over time is the survival skill at all levels of society: the world level; the business organization level; and the individual person level.

Speaking scientifically, the need for the world to maximize its problem solving skill over time is stated by The Supreme Prediction. Here is the The Supreme Prediction:

> Prediction ID# = [P1.0]
> UP_{MAX} will be established and maintained because it is necessary for human survival.

And here is prediction [PHAS6.1] which predicts the necessity of UW Theory education:

> Prediction ID# = [PHAS6.1]
> A UW Theory Education application will be established and maintained because it is necessary for human survival.

Two online courses, one on UP Skill, and one on UW Theory, are already available. So Prediction PHAS 6.1 has already been confirmed!

Transitioning to the New World

An implementation plan is necessary to put UW Theory into practice so that the new world can be realized. Remember that Chapter 3 *The Practice of UW* is only a theory of the practice of UW. The PSAs identified in UW Theory still need to be successfully performed in order for the human survival problem to be solved.

The implementation plan starts with UW Theory education so that people will know the correct actions to take before taking any action, and people can begin to maximize their problem solving skill over time.

The first step in UW Theory education is for everyone to take the beginner Ultimate Person course on the skill of maximum problem solving skill over time and become a Certified Ultimate Person. This free certification course is already established and available now at www.ultimateperson.com.

The next step is for people to take the advanced course on UW Theory. This advanced course is entitled The Ultimate World course and is also available now at www.ultimateperson.com. This book serves as the textbook for The Ultimate World course.

Once people learn the do or die actions identified by UW Theory, they can begin performing them in mainstream business organizations. Once business organizations know what actions to take, then they can begin creating jobs. A Space Life economy is the economy of the future. We need to rethink today's economy as a Space Life economy that is in Earth mode. The Space Life economy has a much larger scope, namely, the scope of the universe as a whole.

One of the biggest and most important projects of the new world will be the Human Survival Problem Solver (HSPS). It will require a vast amount of computer technology skill and resources. One of the biggest tasks associated with building the HSPS is populating the knowledge bases with expert human knowledge in all fields, and in computer security and safety.

The basic design of the HSPS has already been completed and is specified by the HSPS characterizations and hypotheses (see pages 40-62 of this book). This basic design provides a nice jump start to HSPS development.

Finally, an administrative organization with world level authority needs to oversee, and carefully regulate, all of the Ultimate World development and implementation.

Short Term Incentive

Although there is no imminent threat to human survival, there is a significant short term incentive to put UW Theory into real world practice. The short term incentive is to solve all the world's social problems, including the most serious problems that never get solved such as war, violence, hate, and poverty. Most scientists believe the artificial threats to human survival, especially the threat of nuclear warfare, is the greatest threat to human survival.

And there is a long list of other social problems including: poverty; racism; and sexism; that will finally get solved by putting UW Theory into practice. All these social problems will get solved because everyone will be working together as a problem solving team, and all conflict between humans will be eliminated. The simple solution to all these social problems is for everyone to become a certified Ultimate Person by taking the UP Skill course now available at www.ultimateperson.com. This UP Skill course implements this simple solution to all the world's problems free of charge to the world. The sooner people begin taking this course, the sooner these social problems will get solved. The course textbook for the UP Skill is entitled *The Ultimate Person*. The ebook version of *The Ultimate Person* is also available free of charge at www.ultimateperson.com.

Business organizations also have a major short term incentive to put UW Theory into practice. These corporations will need to maximize their group problem solving skill over time to maintain competitiveness. The business organizations that are slow to maximize their group problem solving skill will not survive due to their inability to compete in the marketplace.

And finally, individuals who are slow to maximize their individual problem solving skill will also have difficulty competing in the job market.

An Optimistic Outlook For Human Survival

In closing, the world has good reason to be optimistic about the future. We now have UW Theory which is a good starting point for the world of the future. We now have a method for identifying the do or die actions for the surviving the universe. And we now have a process for maximizing performance and happiness on these do or die actions.

We will be addressing the natural threats to human survival imposed by the universe in the most productive way. And the artificial threats to survival from human conflict will automatically get resolved because everyone will be working together as a problem solving team to address the natural threats. And the Ultimate World will be realized.

APPENDECES

Appendix A. Core Science References

A1. The Basic Scientific Method
A2. Control Theory
A3. Flow Theory
A4. Efficiency Theory
A5. Artificial Intelligence Theory

Appendix B. Boundary Issues

Appendix C. Glossary

Appendix D. Key Diagrams

D1. Ultimate Person Theory
D2. Ultimate World Theory

THE BASIC
SCIENTIFIC METHOD

The scientific method is a collection of techniques for investigating phenomena, acquiring new knowledge, or correcting and integrating previous knowledge. Although there are different ways of outlining the basic method used for scientific inquiry, the scientific community generally agrees on the following classification of method elements:

1) *Characterizations* – definitions, observations, and measurements of the subject of inquiry
2) *Hypotheses* – theoretical explanations of the characterizations
3) *Predictions* – logical deductions from the hypotheses
4) *Experiments* – tests of all of the above

The process of performing science is an iterative process of cycling through these four steps. Over time, the goal is to generate greater accuracy, reliability, objectivity and testability. A scientific theory is the actual hypothesis or set of hypotheses.

THE BASIC SCIENTIFIC METHOD

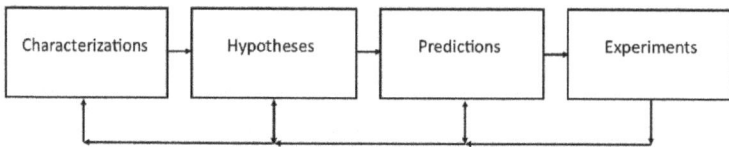

| Characterizations | → | Hypotheses | → | Predictions | → | Experiments |

The basic scientific method diagram illustrates the four steps of the method and the iterative nature of cycling through the steps.

This basic scientific method was the method used in many of the greatest scientific achievements in history. Here are three examples: the Structure of DNA; General Relativity; and the cause and effect relationship of smoking and lung cancer.

The Structure of DNA

The discovery of the structure of Deoxyribonucleic Acid (DNA) is surely one of the greatest scientific achievements. James Watson and Francis Crick jointly discovered in 1953 that the underlying structure of DNA is a double helix. This double helical structure describes the structure of living genetic information and how it is passed on through inheritance. Here are the elements of the scientific method used by Watson and Crick:

DNA Characterizations – a) DNA contains genetic information; b) DNA structures could be observed using X-ray diffraction; and c) a mathematical formula for x-shaped pattern diffraction from helical structures.

DNA Hypothesis – DNA is structured as a double helix.

DNA Predictions – a) If DNA had a double helical structure, its X-ray diffraction pattern would be x-shaped, and b) a double helical structure provides a means for gene replication.

DNA Experiments – a) Pure DNA was crystalized, X-rayed, and its X-ray diffraction pattern showed an x-shape, and b) physical models of the DNA nucleotides were constructed.

The experiments demonstrated that the DNA structure is truly a double helix. Watson and Crick were awarded the Nobel Prize in Physiology or Medicine in 1962.

General Relativity

General Relativity is the geometric theory of gravitation published by Albert Einstein in 1915. General relativity generalizes special relativity and Isaac Newton's law of universal gravitation, providing a unified description of gravity as a geometric property of space and time. The relation is specified by Einstein's field equations.

Here are the elements of the basic scientific method used by Einstein:

General Relativity Characterizations –
a) Special relativity – predicts the equivalence of mass and energy in the following equation:

$$E = mc^2$$

where E is the energy of a particle, m is its mass, and c is the speed of light in a vacuum. Special relativity is considered special because it only applies when gravitational effects are negligible.

b) Newton's universal law of gravitation – a general physical law that states that the force of attraction between two particles is directly proportional to the product of their masses, and inversely proportional to the square of the distance between their centers. It is measured in the following equation:

$$F = \frac{Gm_1m_2}{r^2}$$

where F is the gravitational force acting between two objects, m_1 and m_2 are the masses of the objects, r is the distance between the two objects and G is the gravitational constant.

c) Einstein's field equations – a set of 10 equations that describe the fundamental interaction of gravitation as a result of spacetime being curved by mass and energy. These equations are also known as the mathematics of general relativity.

General Relativity Hypothesis – the curvature of space time is directly related to the energy and momentum of whatever matter and radiation are present.

General Relativity Predictions – a) the gravitational time delay; b) the gravitational lensing (bending of light); c) gravitational waves.

General Relativity Experiments – a) the Hubble telescope showed that galaxies move in a way that confirms general relativity; b) solar eclipses demonstrate the bending of light; c) gravitational waves have been observed using the

Laser Interferometer Gravitational Wave Observatory (LIGO).

The predictions of general relativity have been confirmed in all observations and experiments to date. General relativity stands as the current description of gravitation in modern physics and is often considered the most beautiful of all existing physical theories. Einstein received the 1921 Nobel Prize in Physics for his services in theoretical physics.

The Cause/Effect of Smoking and Lung Cancer

The cause/effect relationship between smoking and lung cancer is a classic example of a scientific cause/effect relationship. It is now well known that tobacco smoking is main contributor to lung cancer. Tobacco smoke contains a long list of carcinogens and smoking is directly linked to the vast majority of lung cancer cases (85%). Here are the elements of the scientific method applied to the cause/effect relationship of smoking and lung cancer:

> *Smoking/lung cancer Characterizations* – a) tobacco smoke contains many carcinogens; b) smoking is directly linked to the vast majority of lung cancer cases (85%); c) data gathering and analysis by the medical community and the Center for Disease Control.

> *Smoking/lung cancer Hypothesis* – smoking causes lung cancer

> *Smoking/lung cancer Prediction* – if you smoke over a long period of time, you are at a very high risk of getting lung cancer.

Smoking/lung cancer Experiments – extensive data gathering by the medical community and the Center for Disease Control confirms the cause/effect relationship of smoking and lung cancer.

Due to the clear link between smoking and lung cancer, numerous restrictions and disincentives are in place. These include designated smoking areas that are away from the general public, heavy "sin" taxes on tobacco products, and doctor's orders to stop smoking.

Relevance To Ultimate World Theory

The Basic Scientific Method is relevant to UW Theory as the underlying method for the UW scientific method. The UW scientific method is derived directly from the four step iterative process of characterizations, hypotheses, predictions, and experiments. It adapts this basic method to the UW context and the UW problem of surviving the universe using minimum resources. The Basic Scientific Method has been well-established for centuries. Using it carefully ensures that UW Theory is truly scientific.

CONTROL THEORY

Control theory is a general theory of feedback systems. The overall theme of control theory is the use of feedback to maintain stability in a system over time. It originated in engineering and mathematics, and evolved into use by the social sciences, such as economics, psychology, and sociology. The theoretical basis for control theory was first described by James Clerk Maxwell in 1868 and has since gone through a number of refinements.

A system is a generic entity for something that takes inputs, processes the inputs in some fashion, and then produces a desired result called an output. The word "system" is a generic term that could apply to anything that processes inputs. For example, a food processor is a system for processing ingredients from a recipe (the input) into finished food ready for consumption (the output). A common application of a food processor is fresh salsa. The ingredients of fresh salsa include tomatoes, onions, garlic, chili peppers, and cilantro. The food processor (the system) chops and blends the ingredients (the inputs) which produces the desired result of fresh salsa (the output).

A SYSTEM

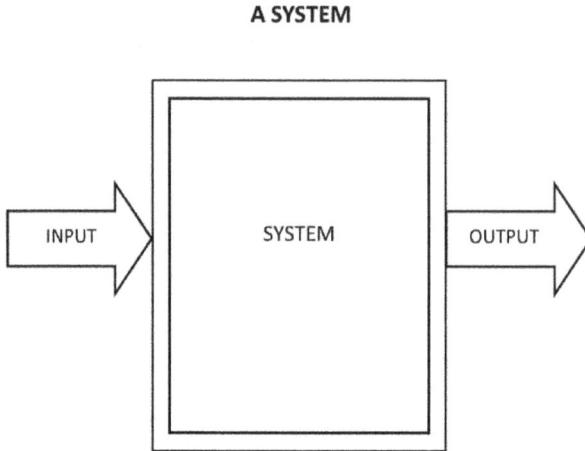

This system diagram illustrates the three elements of a generic system: the input, the output, and the system.

A control system takes the output of a system, uses this output as feedback and makes corrections to the output based a desired goal, called a reference. The control element is called the controller. Notice in the control system diagram that the output is fed back into the controller which compares the actual output to the reference (the desired output), and makes corrections to the output signal which is then input back to the system in a continuous cycle. Stability over time is achieved by using the feedback to make corrections to any variance between the actual output and the desired output. Over time, the variance between the actual output and the desired output is reduced until the desired output is achieved.

A CONTROL SYSTEM

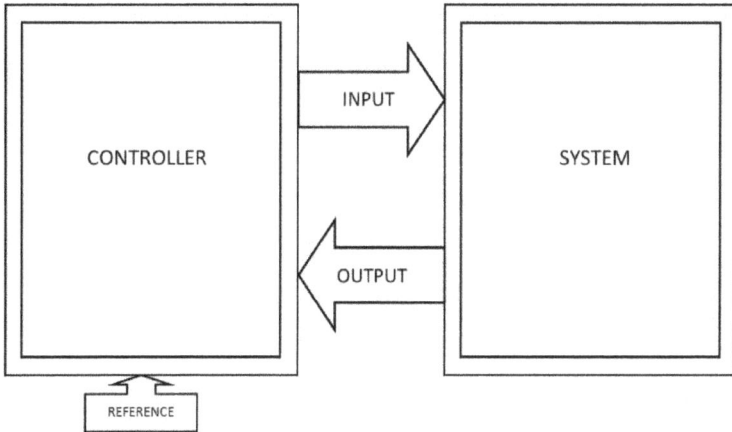

This control system diagram illustrates the framework of the five elements of a control system: the reference, the controller, the input, the output, and the system.

Here are three typical examples of the application of control theory: a temperature control system, a speed control system, and a health control system.

A Temperature Control System

All modern buildings have temperature control systems, implemented in the form of a thermostat. The thermostat allows the user to set a desired temperature and it automatically controls the actual temperature of the building to match the desired temperature set by the user. The five control system elements of a temperature control system are:

1) the reference – the desired temperature set by the user
2) the controller – the electronic control device of the heating, ventilation, air conditioning (HVAC) unit

3) the input – the on/off signal to the heater or air conditioner within the HVAC unit
4) the output – the actual temperature of the air in the room
5) the system – the HVAC unit

Stability over time is achieved by establishing and maintaining the desired temperature set by the user.

A Speed Control System

Most modern cars have speed control systems, implemented in the form of cruise control. A cruise control system allows the driver to set a desired speed and it automatically controls the actual speed of the car to match the desired speed. The five control system elements of a cruise control system are:

1) the reference – the desired speed set by the driver
2) the controller – the electronic control device of the fuel injector
3) the input – the fuel
4) the output – the actual speed of the car
5) the system – the engine

Stability over time is achieved by establishing and maintaining the desired speed set by the driver.

A Health Control System

A common first line diagnostic test done by doctors when patients visit with symptoms of an illness, is the comprehensive metabolic panel (CMP). This lab test gives the doctor critical feedback on the patient's health based on a long list of heath variables such as glucose (blood sugar), and various nutrients (e.g. sodium). The doctor then controls the patient's health condition by prescribing medicine to bring the patient's health variables within the desired ranges. The five control system elements of this health control system are:

1) the reference – the desired ranges of the comprehensive metabolic panel (CMP)
2) the controller – the doctor
3) the input – the patient's blood sample
4) the output – the patient's laboratory report
5) the system – the laboratory

Stability over time is achieved by establishing and maintaining the desired ranges of the CMP.

Relevance to Ultimate World Theory

Control theory is relevant to UW Theory by providing the framework for the interaction between The Technology (the Human Survival Problem Solver), and The People (the Ultimate World). Note that the word "control" and "controller" in UW Theory are actually about maintaining "stability over time" in the Ultimate World. They are not about controlling people in an oppressive sense.

The Control Theory Framework provides a useful feedback mechanism for correcting mistakes, adapting to change, dealing with unknowns, and improving action performance and happiness for both individuals and groups. And it helps ensure that problem solving skill *over time* is maximized. Control theory implements the concept of *time* in UW Theory.

FLOW THEORY

Flow theory describes a mental state during performance of an action in which a person performing the action is fully immersed in a feeling of energized focus, full involvement and enjoyment in the process of the activity. The definitive book on Flow Theory is entitled *Flow: The Psychology of Optimal Experience*. Optimal experience is commonly known as the emotion called maximum happiness – the most positive of all emotions.

Mihaly Csikszentmihalyi is the author of Flow theory. He first published the concept of Flow in psychology in 1975, and then authored the definitive book mentioned above in 1990. He did extensive interviews and monitoring of people performing different types of activities in the search for the conditions of optimal experience. He found that there were three primary conditions of optimal experience:

1) *clear goals* – this provides the necessary structure and direction to the activity

2) *clear and immediate feedback* – this helps the person negotiate any challenging demands and allows them to make adjustments to their performance to maintain a flow state

3) *a balance between challenge and skill* – this balance provides a feeling of confidence and control over one's ability to succeed.

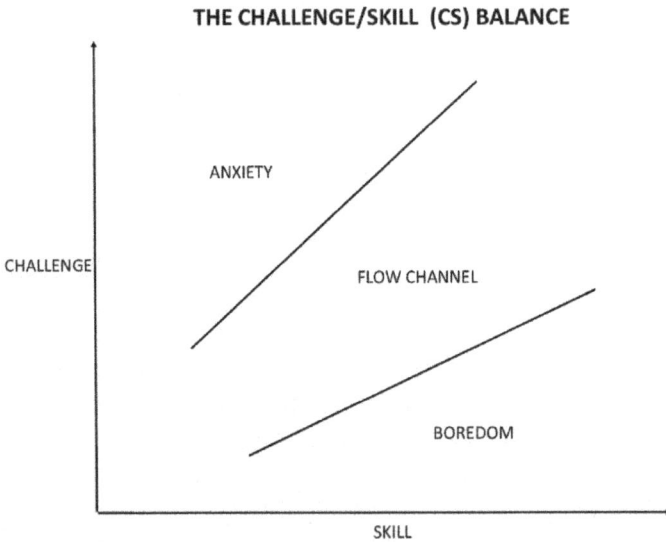

THE CHALLENGE/SKILL (CS) BALANCE

This challenge/skill balance diagram illustrates how the different levels of challenge and skill affect one's mental state.

The challenge/skill balance, or CS Balance, is the golden rule of Flow. The above chart illustrates the CS balance. It is a chart of the challenge level of a certain action versus the skill level available to meet the challenge. Notice that an activity that has high challenge and low skill leads to a state of anxiety or being stressed out because the action cannot be performed. Anxiety has a negative effect on performance because it can cause frustration with an activity that will eventually cause a person to give up and quit the activity.

An activity with low challenge and high skill leads to a state of boredom because the activity is too easily performed. Boredom has a negative effect on performance because it can cause a person to lose interest and eventually quit the activity. In both states – anxiety and boredom – the key performance problem is lost attention and focus on the activity.

By contrast, the CS balance or "flow channel" has a positive effect on performance because a person is succeeding at an activity and increasing skill over time, so that higher levels of performance can be achieved over time. In a Flow state, attention and focus on the activity are maximized.

Examples of Flow

By applying Flow theory to virtually any activity, both performance and happiness can be improved. Here are three examples of applying Flow theory: in sports, in music, and at work.

Flow In Sports

Sports offers plenty of opportunity to experience Flow. Here is how the three primary conditions of Flow apply to sports:

1) clear goals – win the game
2) clear and immediate feedback – the score of the game
3) CS Balance – improving the score by applying athletic skill. This also leads to increased enjoyment of the sport.

Athletes are known to use the following expressions to describe the Flow state: "in the zone," "unbeatable," and "on auto."

Flow In Music

Music also offers plenty of opportunity to experience Flow. Here is how the three primary conditions of Flow apply to music:

1) clear goals – the song's melody (structure) of musical notes
2) clear and immediate feedback – the actual sound of the musical instruments
3) CS Balance – improving the sound by applying musical skill. This also leads to increased enjoyment of the music.

Musicians are known to use the following expressions to describe the Flow state: "perfect harmony," "tuned in," and "jamming."

Flow At Work

Work also offers plenty of opportunity to experience Flow. Here is how the three primary conditions of Flow apply to work:

1) clear goals – performance targets such as sales and customer service ratings
2) clear and immediate feedback – actual performance results on the targets
3) CS Balance – improved performance on the targets by applying the skills of the workers. This also leads to increased enjoyment at work.

Businesses use the following expressions to describe the Flow state: "hit the mark," "better than expected earnings," and "crushing it."

Group Flow

Flow theory also applies to groups. Here is how the three primary conditions of Flow, apply to groups:

1) clear goals – the group goal
2) clear and immediate feedback – the group's performance results
3) CS Balance – improving the performance of the group by applying the skills of the group members. This also leads to increased enjoyment of the group experience.

Sports teams, music bands, business organizations, and virtually any group can benefit significantly from applying Flow Theory.

Relevance to Ultimate World Theory

Flow Theory is relevant to UW Theory by means of the Ultimate Person Performance Process, and is directly integrated into the performance rules. The performance rules for both individuals and groups are justified by their necessity to facilitate a Flow experience.

Flow theory clearly demonstrates the link between action performance and emotional experience. UW Theory shows how Flow theory can be integrated into the Control Theory Framework so that feedback can be used to maintain Flow over time. UW Theory shows how the entire world can stay in Flow over time while solving the human survival problem and therefore, live happily ever after.

EFFICIENCY THEORY

Efficiency is the extent to which time and effort is well used for an intended task or purpose. Efficiency theory is a theory of the measurement of a certain output (the intended task or purpose), in relation to a certain input (time and effort). It is measured as the ratio of output to input in the following equation:

$$Efficiency = Output/Input$$

Efficiency is increased by either increasing output for a given input, or decreasing input for a given output. It is maximized by maximizing the output, and minimizing the input.

Examples of Efficiency Theory

Fuel Efficiency

Perhaps the most common application of efficiency theory is fuel efficiency in automobiles, which is measured in miles per gallon (MPG). The mathematical equation for fuel efficiency is as follows:

Fuel Efficiency = Miles/Gallon

The output of an automobile is the distance traveled measured in miles, and the input is gasoline measured in one gallon. Efficient cars have high miles per gallon, and inefficient cars have low miles per gallon.

There are stringent regulations for fuel efficiency because of the problems associated with inefficient cars such as smog and ozone degradation which can cause serious health problems.

Solar Panel Efficiency

Solar panel efficiency refers to the portion of energy in the form of sunlight that can be converted into electricity. The mathematical equation for solar panel efficiency is:

Solar Panel Efficiency = kWh/m^2

The output of a solar panel is electricity measured in kilowatt hours (kWh). The input is the size of the solar cell panel used to collect sunlight measured in square meters (m^2). As of December 2014, the world record for solar cell efficiency at 46% was achieved by using multi-junction concentrator solar cells.

The development of affordable, inexhaustible and clean solar energy technologies will have huge long term benefits for the world. It will increase energy security, enhance sustainability, reduce pollution, and keep fossil fuel prices much lower than otherwise.

Production Efficiency

Production efficiency refers the amount of product that can be produced from a given labor force. The mathematical equation for production efficiency is:

$$\text{Production Efficiency} = \frac{\text{Number of products produced}}{\text{Number of employees}}$$

An example of production efficiency is the assembly line, which was introduced by Henry Ford. The production of cars was greatly improved by using an assembly line in which each worker performed a specific operation and then sent the car to the next worker. The net result is that more cars were produced using the same workforce.

Relevance to Ultimate World Theory

Efficiency theory applies to UW Theory in the definition of the UW scientific problem specified in Chapter 2. The UW scientific problem is stated in terms of Maximum UW efficiency and is measured as follows:

$$\text{Maximum UW Efficiency} = \frac{UP_{MAX}}{PSA_{MIN}}$$

The overall output of UW theory is Ultimate People (UP), and the overall input of UW theory is Problem Solving Actions (PSA). Maximizing UW efficiency is accomplished by maximizing the number of Ultimate People (UP_{MAX}) and minimizing the number of Problem Solving Actions (PSA_{MIN}).

ARTIFICIAL INTELLIGENCE THEORY

Artificial Intelligence (AI) is a branch of computer science that focuses on the use of computer technology to emulate human intelligence. AI was founded as an academic discipline in 1956, at a workshop at Dartmouth College. The attendees were Nobel Laureate Herbert Simon, Allen Newell, John McCarthy, Marvin Minsky and Arthur Samuel. These attendees became the founders and leaders of AI research. The initial AI applications were using computers to play the game checkers, solving word problems in algebra, proving logical theorems and speaking English.

The overall research goal of AI is to create general intelligence. The general problem of simulating intelligence has been broken down into sub-problems such as problem-solving, planning, and natural language processing.

One of the most successful implementations of AI software is Expert Systems. Expert systems emulate the decision-making ability of a human expert. They are designed to solve complex problems by reasoning about knowledge, represented mainly as IF-THEN rules rather than through conventional procedural code. IF-THEN rules have the advantage of bridging the gap between computer programmers and general human experts. IF-THEN rules are more intuitive and easily understood by general human experts than computer code, but can also be easily coded into the computer software. Edward Feigenbaum, who was one of Herbert Simon's students at Carnegie Mellon University, is known as the author of Expert Systems.

An Expert System has three primary components:

> a) a knowledge base for representing knowledge as facts and rules,
> b) an inference engine which is software that applies the facts and rules to assist the user and to expand the knowledge base,
> c) a user interface which is a computer display that facilitates user interaction with the inference engine and knowledge base.

Human Programming vs. Machine Programming

Since its inception in the 1950s, numerous AI techniques have been developed which can be classified into two basic types: *human-programmed and machine-programmed. Human-programmed* AI techniques are characterized by explicit programming by a human being. An example of an human-programmed AI technique is Expert Systems. *Machine-programmed* AI techniques are characterized by having the machine program the system on its own without explicit programming by a human. An example of a machine-programmed AI technique is Machine Learning.

There is a major safety issue involved in using machine-programmed AI systems to address human survival problems because it would allow the computer to determine human survival knowledge, and make human survival decisions on its own. Everyone's fear that machines will gain control over humans — and then terminate us (as in the Terminator movie series) — could be realized. Therefore, machine-programmed AI techniques need to be carefully restricted and regulated for use on human survival problems.

The Human Survival Problem Solver (HSPS) is a human-programmed AI system because it requires programming by human experts. The HSPS falls into the AI category of "problem solving expert system."

Relevance to Ultimate World Theory

AI theory applies to UW Theory by means of the Human Survival Problem Solver. The HSPS is an intelligent computer system based on Expert Systems technology (a human-programmed AI technique), and serves as the controller for the Ultimate World and Ultimate Person control systems. Over time, new AI techniques will be developed and implemented into the Human Survival Problem Solver. However, for safety reasons, machine-programmed AI techniques need to be carefully restricted. This is especially true for the HSPS because it deals with human survival knowledge. In the HSPS, machine-programming is secondary to human-programming.

BOUNDARY ISSUES

This section entitled *boundary issues* fits the theme of credible communication throughout this book. A boundary issue is an issue that UW Theory does not address. It is part of the diligent effort of carefully wording everything to avoid any confusion over what is addressed and what is not addressed by UW Theory. This way the information presented can be relied upon. There are six boundary issues:

1) UW Theory is not a complete solution to the human survival problem. The problem of surviving the universe using minimum resources is so complex, it is virtually impossible to define all the details all at one time. The human survival solution is an ongoing journey and UW Theory is just the starting point. As given in the introduction, UW Theory is a good starting point because it correctly defines the big issues, and provides a method for defining the remaining details.

2) *Chapter 3 The Practice of the Ultimate World* is only a theory of the practice of UW. It only specifies how the PSAs need to be performed in order to maximize performance results and happiness. Be sure to consult local professionals, including legal and financial professionals, before putting anything in UW Theory into actual practice.

3) The term "future-proof" is used to describe one of the benefits of learning UW Theory. Future-proofing a person refers to acquiring the skills necessary to compete in the job market over time (namely, maximizing problem solving skill over time). It does not refer to future proofing a person's life.

4) This book does not address specific hardware and software implementations for the Human Survival Problem Solver. It is limited to the necessary design elements and the necessary information flows between the elements. Hardware and software implementations for the Human Survival Problem Solver are certainly necessary. However, hardware and software technology changes frequently over time, and is beyond the scope of this book.

5) The predictions given in *Chapter 5 Summary of the UW Predictions* do not guarantee specific times or dates. They only predict that they will occur in the future because they are necessary for human survival. However, time deadlines are given in the characterizations for each PSA to encourage efficient completion.

6) The math in this initial edition of UW Theory only specifies maximum and minimum values for UPs and PSAs. Calculating specific numbers for UP_{MAX} and PSA_{MIN} is extremely difficult. However, there are success measures given in the characterizations of the PSAs. Some are quantified, and some are not. These success measures can be used to determine whether a PSA has been successfully completed or not.

GLOSSARY

artificial intelligence (AI): a branch of computer science that focuses on the use of computer technology to emulate human intelligence

basic scientific method: a method for investigating phenomena, acquiring new knowledge, or correcting and integrating previous knowledge. It has four basic steps: characterizations; hypotheses; predictions; and experiments

challenge/skill balance: a feeling of confidence and control over one's ability to succeed. It is also known as the golden rule of Flow theory

characterization: a definition; observation; or measurement within a scientific study. UW Theory characterizations consist of a list of eleven data fields

control theory: a general theory of feedback systems. The overall theme is the use of feedback to maintain stability in a system over time

control theory framework (CTF): a framework based on the five elements of a control system – reference; controller; input; output; and system

experiment: a test on a characterization, hypothesis, or prediction within a scientific study. The majority of experiments are tests on hypotheses

expert system: an artificial intelligence technique designed to solve complex problems by reasoning about knowledge, represented mainly as IF-THEN rules rather than conventional procedural code. Expert systems are considered a human-programmed AI technique because the knowledge base is explicitly programmed by a human being, and not implicitly programmed by the computer

feedback: information about a person's performance of a task, which is used as a basis for improvement

flow theory: a psychological theory of optimal experience. It has three primary conditions: clear goals; clear and immediate feedback on progress; and a challenge/skill balance

human extinction: the complete end of the human species

human survival problem solver (HSPS): a world-wide computer based solutions manager for managing all human survival problems in all safe locations of the universe and all time. It is also known as the future of the internet

human survival problem identification application: an HSPS application designed to maximize problem solving skill over time on the problem of human survival problem identification
hypothesis: a theoretical explanation of the characterizations of a scientific study. It is also known as the theory of the study. A UW hypothesis has the following format – [PSA name] is a necessary action because [Reason for necessity]

inference engine: software program for applying a knowledge base to the specific problems that are input through the user interface of an expert system

knowledge base: a collection of knowledge represented in a computer primarily in the form of IF-THEN rules

maximum problem solving skill over time (MPSSOT): the skill of mastering problem solving with continuous improvement over time

necessitive knowledge: a new knowledge type that defines the actions necessary for human survival of the universe. It is also known as "do or die" knowledge for the world

personal problem solving skill: a problem solving skill based on applying MPSSOT to personal issues such as health, finances and family

problem: a threat to the achievement of a goal

professional problem solving skill: a problem solving skill based on applying MPSSOT to your occupation

prediction: a logical deduction from the hypothesis of a scientific study. A UW prediction has the following format – [problem name] will be [action name] because it is necessary for human survival

problem solving action (PSA): an action that is necessary to solve a specific problem within UW theory. A PSA is the basic unit of human behavior in UW Theory

PSA$_{MIN}$: the minimum number of Problem Solving Actions (PSAs)

reason for necessity: a data field within the UW characterizations that provides the specific reasoning for the necessity of a PSA

safety awareness application: an HSPS application designed to maximize problem solving skill over time on the problem of safety awareness

space life economy application: an HSPS application designed to maximize problem solving skill over time on the problem of managing a space life economy

system: a generic term for something that takes inputs, process them, and produces outputs

user interface: an HSPS computer display with three primary elements – user input/output; PSA list; and support

ultimate person (UP): a person who maximizes problem solving skill over time

ultimate person control system: a control system with the following elements – UP reference; UP controller; UP input; UP output; and UP system

ultimate person performance process (UPPP): an ongoing six-step process for maximizing both action performance results and emotional experience (happiness). It adheres to a set of performance rules based on Flow theory

ultimate world (UW): a world-wide group of UPs who work together as a team to maximize group problem solving skill over time

ultimate world control system: a control system with the following elements – UW reference; UW controller; UW input; UW output; and UW system

UP$_{MAX}$: the maximum number of Ultimate People. UP$_{MAX}$ is the key element in the Supreme Hypothesis of UW Theory (in short form – $UW = UP_{MAX}$).

UW theory: a scientific theory of how the entire world can work together as a problem solving team to solve all the world's problems and have fun doing it

UW experiment form: a simple one-page form that facilitates identification of all the necessary information for a credible experiment within UW Theory

UW characterizations: a set of eleven data fields – PSA name, PSA ID#, problem name, problem ID#, action name, reason for necessity, unit of analysis, time deadline, success measure, supplemental definitions, and supplemental reasoning

UW hypotheses: theoretical explanations within UW Theory that have the following format – [PSA name] is a necessary action because [reason for necessity]

UW predictions: a logical deduction from a UW hypothesis. It has the following format – [problem name] will be [action name] because it is necessary for human survival.

UW problem: survive the universe using minimum resources

UW experiments: there are two types of UW experiments– ADD hypothesis, and DELETE hypothesis. The ADD hypothesis is in the following format: [PSA name] is a necessary action because [reason for necessity]. The DELETE hypothesis is in the following format: [PSA name] is not a necessary action because [reason for not-necessity]

UW scientific method: a four step scientific method derived directly from the Basic Scientific Method, adapted to the UW Context and the UW Problem

UW scientific problem: a formula for maximizing UW efficiency. The specific formula is Maximum UW Efficiency = UP_{MAX}/PSA_{MIN}

UW scientific solution: a set of PSAs specified by the set of hypotheses within UW Theory. The initial edition of UW Theory has a total of 70 hypotheses. Therefore, the initial UW scientific solution has 70 PSAs

UW Theory education application: an HSPS application designed to maximize problem solving skill over time on the problem of educating the world on UW Theory and certifying everyone as UPs

KEY DIAGRAMS

Appendix D. Key Diagrams

D1. Ultimate Person Theory Diagram
D2. Ultimate World Theory Diagram

D1. Ultimate Person Theory Diagram

The Ultimate Person Theory Diagram is a key diagram because it illustrates the skill of maximum problem solving skill over time – the survival skill of the future. It shows the UP inputs, the UP outputs, and the UP system for processing the inputs, and producing the outputs. The UP system is the Ultimate Person Performance Process which guides each person toward maximum performance and maximum happiness. This diagram represents the basic problem solving unit of the world of the future. The Ultimate World Theory Diagram shows how all these problem solving units fit together in the Ultimate World.

ULTIMATE PERSON THEORY

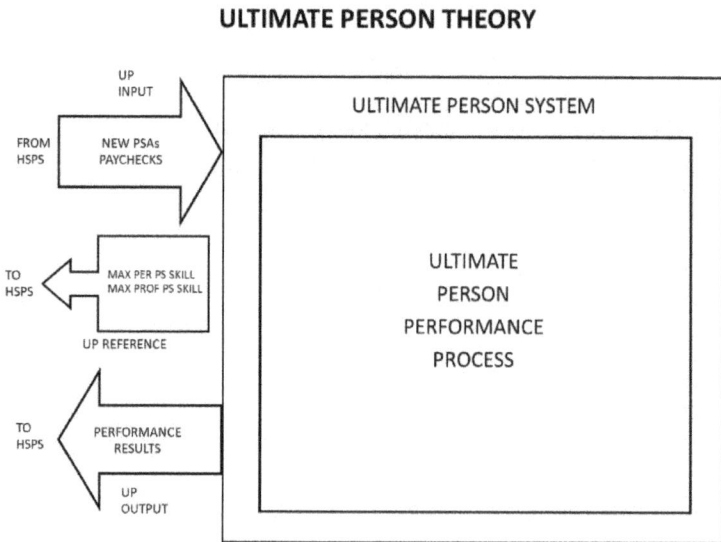

UP INPUT

FROM HSPS

NEW PSAs PAYCHECKS

ULTIMATE PERSON SYSTEM

TO HSPS

MAX PER PS SKILL
MAX PROF PS SKILL

UP REFERENCE

ULTIMATE
PERSON
PERFORMANCE
PROCESS

TO HSPS

PERFORMANCE RESULTS

UP OUTPUT

D2. Ultimate World Theory Diagram

The Ultimate World Theory Diagram is a key diagram because it represents an informational road map for the entire UW Theory. If a person gets lost or confused while learning a detailed element within UW Theory, they can just zoom out to this diagram to find where they are. This diagram is the big picture on UW Theory. Interestingly, this diagram represents the solution to all the world's problems, all on one page.

ULTIMATE WORLD THEORY

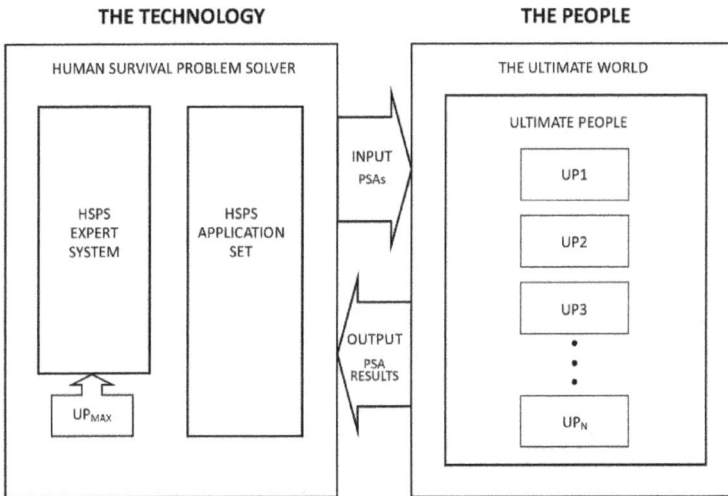

ABOUT THE AUTHOR

Carmen Tripodi is the ultimate authority on the ultimate topics. The two ultimate topics are The Ultimate Person and The Ultimate World.   His credibility as an ultimate authority is established by his accurate and reliable definitions of each of these two ultimate topics. His definitions are accurate and reliable, and therefore correct, because they are based on science.

These definitions are detailed in Carmen's two companion books entitled *The Ultimate Person* and *The Ultimate World.*

Now that the scientific definitions of The Ultimate Person and The Ultimate World are available, everyone can now take the steps to become a true Ultimate Person, and The Ultimate World can now be realized. Above all, all the world's problems can now be solved.

Carmen teaches two online courses at www.ultimateperson.com. The first course is a free beginner course that teaches the ultimate skill of *maximum problem solving skill over time*, and certifies people as an Ultimate Person. The first course actually implements the simple solution to all the world's problems, free of charge to the world. The second course is an advanced course that teaches the underlying science of The Ultimate Person and The Ultimate World, and certifies students as an expert on these ultimate topics.

His primary contribution to science is the development of Ultimate World Theory, the scientific theory that saves the world. Ultimate World Theory, along with many other scientific innovations, is detailed in *The Ultimate World.*

He also invented (patent pending) the Human Survival Problem Solver, which is also known as the future of the internet. The Human Survival Problem Solver will play an essential role in The Ultimate World, much in the same way the present day internet plays an essential role in the present day world.

Education

Carmen has a Master of Science degree in Computer Information Systems from Claremont Graduate University, and a

Bachelor of Science degree in Electrical Engineering from Pennsylvania State University. He has also taken enough Psychology courses, at both the graduate and undergraduate levels, to informally qualify as having a minor in Psychology.

www.ingramcontent.com/pod-product-compliance
Lightning Source LLC
Chambersburg PA
CBHW022104280326
41933CB00007B/254